Provençal Escapes

Provençal Escapes

inspirational homes in Provence and the Côte d'Azur

CAROLINE CLIFTON-MOGG

with photography by Christopher Drake

RYLAND
PETERS
& SMALL

LONDON NEW YORK

SENIOR DESIGNER Sally Powell
SENIOR EDITOR Henrietta Heald
PICTURE AND LOCATION RESEARCH
Emily Westlake
PRODUCTION Sheila Smith
ART DIRECTOR Gabriella Le Grazie
PUBLISHING DIRECTOR Alison Starling

First published in 2005 by
Ryland Peters & Small
20–21 Jockey's Fields
London WC1R 4BW

Ryland Peters & Small, Inc.
519 Broadway, 5th Floor
New York, NY 10012
www.rylandpeters.com

This paperback edition published 2009.

10 9 8 7 6 5 4 3 2 1

ISBN 978 1 84597 855 6

A CIP record for this book is available from
the British Library.

The original US edition of this book was
cataloged as follows:

Library of Congress Cataloging-in-Publication Data
Clifton-Mogg, Caroline.
  Provencal escapes : inspirational homes in
Provence and the Côte d'Azur / Caroline Clifton-
Mogg ; with photography by Chris Drake.
      p. cm.
  Includes index.
  ISBN 1-84172-934-5
1. Provence (France)--Social life and customs--
Pictorial works. 2. Provence (France)--Description
and travel--Pictorial works. 3. Dwellings--France--
Provence--Pictorial works. 4. Architecture, Domestic
--France--Provence--Pictorial works. 5. Interior
decoration--France--Provence--Pictorial works.
6. Lifestyles--France--Provence--Pictorial works.
7. France, Southern--Description and travel--
Pictorial works. I. Drake, Chris, 1950- II. Title.
  DC611.P958C58 2005
  747'.0944'9--dc22
                                          2005002959

Printed and bound in China.

contents

introduction

There is some dispute about how much of southern France can actually be called Provence. Although all agree that from the north it runs from Montélimar down to the sea, some say that the eastern border lies just east of Aix-en-Provence, while others insist that it stretches to the edge of the Alpes-Maritimes. The one thing on which all Provence lovers agree, however, is that somewhere beyond Lyons, probably between Montélimar and Orange, there is a moment when the light visibly changes, and the air becomes softer and warmer and filled with the evanescent scents of lavender, rosemary and pine and the energetic sound of cicadas. This is the starting point for those who know that Provence is not simply a geographical area of whatever dimensions but, more importantly, a state of mind, a place where one can escape from the grey routine of daily life into another gayer, brighter world.

For it is the case that each one of us, at some time, needs to escape, or, at the very least, to dream of escaping, to a more generous place; and, although not everyone dreams of escaping to exactly the same location, for many the ideal sanctuary must have elements of beauty, comfort and pleasure, and should preferably also be a place where the days are warm and long, the scenery both varied and captivating, and where many of life's small pleasures can be found in abundance. It is not surprising, therefore, that so many people choose to make their escape to the warm embrace of Provence.

Provençal Escapes is about the sort of house in which many of us dream of living, and in which some actually do. Not all the houses that feature in this book are part-time refuges; some have full-time owners, those lucky people who have managed to plan the great escape and are now enjoying the fruits of their planning.

The idea of the Provençal house appeals to an almost basic need in many of us. Perhaps we see in our mind's eye a traditional, old stone house with wooden shutters at the windows and a long terrace, shaded by fig and olive trees and surrounded with terracotta pots of rosemary and lavender – a place redolent of the joys of simple summer life. Of course, not all escapist houses in Provence are like that – in fact, few are. They come in all shapes, sizes and types; some are luxurious, some simple. Luxury does not make an escape but, equally, luxury is no barrier, and there is no particular virtue in simplicity for simplicity's sake.

An escape can be small or large; it can be on the side of a mountain or in a field, on a hill overlooking the sea or hidden in a wood; it can be of any age – some of our escapes are 200 or 300 years old, others are modern. Some are surrounded by land; others are in medieval villages, surrounded by other houses – though nearly every escape boasts a terrace or roof from which to see the sky. What they all have in common is that, to their owners, these escapes are places where whatever way of life is needed can be found immediately around them – and that is the greatest luxury of all.

simply rustic

The decorative style of Provence is by its very nature both simple and rustic. Traditionally — before tourism and new industries arrived — Provence was a poor region of limited agriculture, which varied from area to area, but which included the herding of sheep and goats and the cultivation of grapes and olives. Local homes, from the grandest *bastide* to the smallest village house, were built with local materials and furnished as simply as was practical. The texture and appearance of the materials used were important — rough-hewn stone, handmade terracotta floor and roof tiles, heavy, wooden beams and limewashed, textured walls. Furniture was made from the wood available in the nearby countryside — in particular walnut, occasionally cherry and olive — and the colours used in decoration imitated the colours of the earth, the tiles, the grass, the olives, the lavender fields. The simplicity of the past is echoed in houses throughout Provence today.

Left At the foot of steps leading down from the street is a cool paved terrace, arranged as an eating area, with a table laid for a shady lunch.

Below and opposite The kitchen has a traditional design but with quirky details such as the wall lights, originally dating from the Empire period. The sink area is surrounded by black tiles, called anciennes de Salerne, *made in the town of Salerne, the centre of Provençal tile making. An old farm table, a 20th-century metal chair from Italy and a collection of 19th-century terracotta and glass complete the picture.*

cool sanctuary

The house that Nelly Guyot owns in Ramatuelle, and the way that she has decorated it, could be interpreted as a textbook example of how to achieve the right look – the right look, that is, for simple, peaceful holidays in the sun.

If you decided to follow, in a general sort of way, the guidance implicitly offered by Nelly Guyot, then, with barely any effort at all, you too could have the perfect holiday house: a place that is cool and calm to live in, ageless and with perfect style – and, even if your own particular haven does not look quite as perfect as Nelly's house, it will still be a very pleasant place to live.

But to begin at the beginning. About eight years ago, Nelly Guyot, Parisian interior designer and lover of the simple style, decided to buy a house in the Provençal village of Ramatuelle. This is a popular village for good reason – it combines both the virtues and beauty of the archetypal fortified medieval hillside village with the more temporal pleasures of the beaches and town life

Above A Catalan table, a metal chair and a military folding seat furnish this comfortable sitting room, once a shelter for sheep; the tapestry cushions are from Chelsea Textiles.

Opposite, above left Beside the stairs is an old, closed French armoire, originally made in two parts for ease of transport.

Opposite, above right An unlikely mixture of objects – including a processional lamp, a Moroccan mirror and a Greek bust – make an harmonious whole.

Opposite, below right An original stone fireplace is flanked by a cushioned stone seat, an English armchair, a small African chair and a low coffee table.

Buildings of this age have their own pace and their own character and personality that it's perilous to meddle with. One must 'respect the style of the house', says Nelly.

of St Tropez. Nelly Guyot came to Ramatuelle to find a traditional *maison de village* – a style that has long been popular for holiday houses, since it is both full of character and yet small enough to be easily cared for. For Nelly, a single *maison de village* would have been too small, so she bought two houses, dating back at least to the 17th century, and converted them into one.

Apart from giving her more space, this arrangement meant that Nelly was able to configure the rooms so that they worked best for her. As it transpired, she didn't alter a great deal. Houses of this age have their own pace and their own character and personality that it is perilous to meddle with.

Two houses meant two kitchens, so she changed the smaller of the two into a study, and embellished and extended the larger one. The main reception room opens onto the terrace and is now *un espace vivant* – a living space. Much of the restoration and repair work that was carried out was utilitarian, introducing new

windows, different stairs. It was, as she says, 'a lot of work to achieve the simple'. Much of it is invisible in the final result, but that is what good design and decoration is all about: the amount of work you put in to achieve the unseen and unnoticed, the work that underpins the foundations, whether literal or metaphorical, is what informs and dictates the ultimate design.

Once the basic remedial work has been completed, says Nelly, the essential thing is to continue to respect the style of the house and ensure that everything decorative should be within that style. For her,

this is not difficult. Her signature is purity of line, and in everything she does a certain aesthetic prevails – not severe, but certainly one without excessive frills or furbelows. For example, the entire house is decorated in a pared-down neutral palette, the better to offset the heat of the Mediterranean summer's day. She uses white and more white, different nuances of the basic colour, sometimes softened with a little cream, occasionally with a little added grey and sometimes yellow – what Nelly calls '*couleurs claires*', which are very different from the colours that she would use in an urban decorative scheme.

Opposite, left, above and below **Showing the charm of simplicity, the beds in this twin room are folding military camp beds, while the mattresses are new, made of wool and covered in cotton and silk. The small red bear, from Russia, sits next to a 1940s glass lamp that belonged to Nelly's grandmother.**

Above and opposite, right **Another simple bedroom, with a bathroom leading off it, is dominated by a 17th-century armoire, which was restored by Nelly to its original beauty. The wall light is converted from a 1940s ceiling light, and the bedside light is an old church candlestick converted to electricity.**

Everything Nelly does, from colour to curtains, is intended to produce a house that is both a refuge and a delight, and which works perfectly.

All the furniture was bought by Nelly specifically for this project. It is old – her preferred style – and follows the rule of simplicity of style and line; some of it is in good condition, some not. Like much old French country furniture, many of the pieces are painted in soft greys and whites, several of them decorated by Nelly. She also bought local Provençal dishes and glassware that would be in keeping with the furniture; they are pieces that can be used every day, including chunky, glazed earthenware and thick, generous glasses – immensely practical as well as good-looking, and made to the same designs for hundreds of years.

When it came to the choice of textiles, someone with such a strong preference for simplicity would have been most unlikely to introduce exotic brocades and printed silks into the decorative scheme. Plain fabrics or stripes are all that she allows. Whether on beds or curtains, cushions or covers, there is no glimmer of a print or intricate weave to be seen.

All this amounts to a textbook lesson in decorating. Nelly Guyot does not deviate from what she sets out to do; she understands the limitations as well as the possibilities of a space, and everything she does, from colour to curtains, is meant to produce a house that is both a refuge and a delight, and which works perfectly.

Above **A Sicilian frame of iron, both wrought and gilded, adds splendour to a bed covered in a spread of traditional courte-pointe.**

Left **Nelly has sought to achieve harmony of tone in every room in the house. Here, the painted chair with its rush seat, the painted wooden table and the antique paper-covered box are all of a piece.**

Opposite **Nothing is quite as it seems in this room. Against the large mirror on the floor – designed as an overmantel mirror – is a 20th-century mirrored commode, known as a meuble de chemise, while the elegant metal chair is in fact the frame of a 19th-century chair, which would normally have been upholstered.**

essential vernacular

Originally a shepherd's dwelling, this stone house near St Paul de Vence has survived several incarnations. In much of this area, traditional rural life continues as it always has, and even today the house has many reminders of the past, such as the old well and the pond on the site of the old drinking trough.

Built into the rock, and still retaining its original façade, the former farm building was first transformed into a domestic dwelling in the 1930s. Bought by the present owners in the 1970s as a holiday home, by the 1990s it needed updating and adapting to meet the new needs of the family, including a generation of grown-up children who wished to use the house in different ways.

This challenging task was undertaken by Andrzej Zarzycki, half of the talented British design team of Collett–Zarzycki, in collaboration with the locally based architect and designer Robert Dallas, who, with his responsive understanding and use of the Provençal vernacular, has restored, renovated and built some of the most sympathetic houses in this part of the world. The redesign of this house was intended to reflect the artisanal, unmechanized way of life pursued there in the past, while making possible the installation or updating of many contemporary necessities – from dealing with the damp to cosmetic niceties such as upgrading the bathrooms. It was important, the designers knew, to retain the existing rustic character of the house, to re-order it without losing its essence.

As is so often the case with such a project, once they began to look carefully at the house, the designers realized that there was far more to do than had originally been planned. Andrzej says, 'We took off the roof, we took out the floors, we added a room, and a new hall to reach that room. Basically, we trashed it!' – which was, of course, very far from what they did.

They set out to use the same materials as had always been used, but occasionally to achieve a balance between modernity and the vernacular building style – an archway, for example, might be made in concrete and then clad in stone. They wanted, as Andrzej says, 'to do new things behind old doors'. The kitchen, which was designed to accommodate free-standing kitchen furniture in the traditional manner,

They set out to use the same materials as had always been used, but occasionally to achieve a balance between modernity and the area's vernacular building style.

Opposite, above and below **As organic in appearance as the house, the interior of the pool room is a necessary haven from the heat of the sun. Neither plastered nor painted, the stone is used for built-in benches as well as for the large lintel of an inglenook fireplace.**

Above **A new barbecue has been fashioned from another area carved from the old stone buildings, including a former well. The barbecue is designed in such a way that the glowing embers from the oak fire in the corner can be shovelled into a specially made barbecue tray.**

and incorporates that most welcoming of features, an enormous fireplace, was kept in the same place as it had occupied before, but it was extended. Indeed, the entire house has been extended by about two metres (six feet), making every room more spacious. An internal laundry room was moved outside and the freed-up space transformed into a private bolt-hole.

To emphasize the feeling of inside–outside living, the large living room was faced in the same stone as that used outside, with a new iron-balustraded staircase constructed in the position of the original one. In other parts of the house, the walls were finished with plaster, sometimes mixed with a coarse sand aggregate, giving a rough, rustic appearance.

Details were important. The chandelier that hangs above the kitchen table holds candles in the traditional way, but hidden in its branches are tiny downlighters that illuminate the table underneath. The bunk beds designed for the children were made in such a way that they could be easily dismantled and transformed into full-size beds, and in the bathroom attached to the

light and airy principal bedroom, the low window has been specially designed and situated so that a bather can see the woods beyond.

They also wanted to open up the house more towards the larger landscape. Traditionally, the windows in old Provençal village houses are small, to minimize the impact of the sometimes fierce winds and to help retain heat in winter. Here, French windows opening onto a terrace were installed, and elsewhere they managed to reuse some of the original wooden windows and to make new ones out of oak, the

traditional building material of the area. Not quite so traditional were the metal window shutters put in by Robert Dallas; they were inserted into the stone walls behind wooden shutters – creating an invisible, yet very effective security device.

Old terracotta tiles were used throughout the house, adding greatly to the sense of calm on every floor. Original curved terracotta tiles – *tuiles canals* – were deemed too expensive to be used for the whole roof; instead, new versions of the shape were laid as a bottom layer,

Above and opposite, right **The principal bedroom is decorated in pale blue, with a new bed designed in traditional style. The soft rose of the old terracotta tiles, and the soothing blue tones of the curtains and walls make this a room of utter peace.**

Opposite, above left **The tongue-and-groove walls in this children's room are made from fourth-grade oak for an instant old look, and the new doors have also been distressed.**

Opposite, below **A bathroom coloured in darker blue tones fits easily into the total decorative scheme.**

with the mellow, antique version above. The designers' concern to replicate the soft colours of the old and the antique meant that they sought to use natural paint colours. 'We looked at what was in nature around us – for example, picking a leaf from an olive tree and using the soft grey-green tones for all the exterior shutters.'

Outside, they designed a dining room beside the swimming pool; what had been in an earlier incarnation an outdoor bar was turned into a seating and eating area – a refuge from the sun during the day and, in the evening, a sheltered place for supper, complete with a deep raised inglenook fireplace.

The garden was laid out by landscape designer Jean Mus. As Andrzej says, 'He has a similar ethos to ours. He is interested in the natural rather than the artificial; he wants to regain the idea of the Mediterranean garden, using the local vegetation and, above all, no imported plants.' The care taken with every aspect of the overall design – particularly the overriding concern with authenticity and tradition – has resulted in a house that will stand the test of time for years to come.

Left and inset **An original stone wall has been painted white to make a room of light and air. The oversized window, hung with unlined white curtains, overlooks the courtyard, and beyond are views of the sea. The dark wood bedhead, carved by a South African artist, is completely in keeping with the overall Mediterranean feel.**

Above **The adjoining bathroom has a low window that allows the bather to look out over the nearby woodland. The windows are fastened with an efficient closing mechanism that makes use of a bar which swings and then fastens into both top and bottom of the window frame.**

This page *Village houses were not designed to have large gardens. The usual solution is a terrace – here a place of charm and comfort, with a bench that continues around the corner and is piled high with cushions in vintage fabrics. Pots of plants are everywhere, from oleander to geranium and verbena.*

Right *A half-door, like a stable door, leads from the street into the main room of the house; although the overall space is small, it has been divided into distinct areas, and the eating area is on the street side.*

haven of peace

Life is fine in Ramatuelle, the medieval hill village above St Tropez, and many of the old houses here have been restored and transformed into doll's houses of delight. One of these belongs to Tita Bay, an Italian interior decorator, in whose hands it has become a doll's house of distinctive chic.

When looking at beautiful photographs of Provençal interiors, it is often hard to realize just how small many of the houses in Provence's medieval fortified villages really are. Take Ramatuelle, for instance, the old hill village above St Tropez. Many of the houses in the twisting, arcaded streets are tiny, with little more than one room on each floor, and lean up, as if for company, against the houses on either side.

In common with other fortified towns in the area, Ramatuelle was invaded and ravaged during the Middle Ages and later – so much so that it was completely reconstructed in 1620 after being destroyed in the Religious Wars – but these days the only invading hordes are the relatively few tourists who have escaped from the crowded streets of nearby St Tropez. It is in Ramatuelle that Tita Bay, an Italian interior

The absence of any sense of claustrophobia in the tiny space is in part due to Tita Bay's sophisticated use of textiles and colours.

Left Striking old black and cream floor tiles unite various spaces in the house. Everything is drawn into the decorative scheme, including the stairs that lead down to the floor below; the retaining wall is used like a display table, and as a place for some of the many cushions that can be seen throughout the house. A trellis-fronted cupboard holds earthenware, and through the doorway can be seen Tita's bedroom with its elaborately draped curtains.

Right In Tita's bedroom, fabric is everywhere – not only at the window, but also draped in voluminous folds over the table.

decorator, has used her own particular doll's house to create a contemporary take on rustic Provençal style, using traditional elements in a highly untraditional way.

On the ground floor, entered from the street through a half stable door, Tita has carved out separate spaces that each have a distinct role yet which combine to make a most harmonious room. In the eating corner, by the window, is a round table covered in a floor-length cloth, while built-in cement seating, strewn with cushions, runs up to the over-sized fireplace. The other side of the fireplace, where the seating continues along the wall, is Tita's reading area, dominated by a comfortable chair drawn up to the hearth.

Tita Bay uses textiles as punctuation points. Both in her bedroom and in the living area, the tables are draped with full, floor-length cloths, the windows are dressed with voluminous, dramatic swathes of unlined fabric, draped and tied in a way more often seen in a high-ceilinged Parisian apartment, and there are cushions everywhere – both inside and outside on

her tiny flower-filled terrace. And yet the effect is not overpowering, particularly since she has avoided using rugs on the floor, preferring to let the old cream and black tiles take centre stage; in fact, the textiles add an air of femininity and comfort without making the space feel stuffy or overdressed.

Colour is her other tool. Although there are patterns in her textile collection, they are soft in tone and repetitive and geometric in design; the overall effect is of metres of soft, creamy fabric fading gently into the background. As for the use of paint, every structural element, from the chimney piece in the living room to the walls and ceiling both there and in the bedrooms – even the built-up sides of the staircase that descends to the lower floor – is painted either white or cream, with no attempt to add contrast or artificial excitement.

This deliberate simplicity, coupled with a feminine love and enjoyment of comfort and relaxation, is why the tiny house of Tita Bay is so successful. Who would not wish to step in off the street, shut the door behind one and sink into one of the comfortable seats, at total peace with the world?

Above **Cushions abound in the built-in seating area near the fireplace, and a comfortable chair, upholstered in stripes, is drawn up close to the fire.**

Top and above right **Ingenuity has been employed in this arrangement of shelf and hanging space – rough pieces of** wood make up the shelf and hanging rail, while the hangers themselves have been made of driftwood and hooks.

Right **A guest bedroom has been made under the eaves, where the old beams dominate. All is pale and discreet, with the exception of the printed zebra rug.**

Main picture and inset **This fine old house, with its russet lime mortar walls and small windows for protection, still looks much as it did two centuries ago. The courtyard garden is dominated by a large, shade-giving tree. A fig flourishes in one corner, and climbing vines are trained along the walls. The cobbled surface is laid in an age-old pattern, and a small metal table and chairs complete the traditional picture.**

tones of the earth

Built more than 200 years ago as a presbytery for the local priest, this beguiling village house encompasses many of the traditional and essential building styles of Provence, and seems almost to emanate from the earth that surrounds it. The design of the roof tiles, for example, dates back to Roman times.

Although the Provençal house – or the idea of it – is seen by many to epitomize the idyll of country life, most of the houses we now admire in this part of France were not, on the whole, built as retreats for lazy summer days. They were working houses – farms, homes for local merchants or, as in this case, a house originally built as a presbytery for the local priest. In style and appearance, these houses were not city houses, which often followed the accepted symmetrical classical tradition, but organic practical dwellings, which were added to as necessary, often resulting in a pleasant asymmetry.

More than two centuries old, this particular village house, lived in for 35 years by the present occupant, encompasses many of the traditional building styles of Provence. It has thick walls and small windows, both of which give protection from the often chilling winds – in particular, the painful mistral, which hurtles down the tunnel of the Rhône Valley. Tellingly, there is only one window on the north side.

This page The interior of the old farmhouse has deliberately been kept as low-key as the exterior. Although the present owner made some necessary changes, especially in the rationalizing of spaces and elimination of partitions, the overall effect is one of changes carried out gradually over time, heightened by details such as the antique 'push me-pull you' light.

Right **Classic farmhouse chairs with angled backs, rush seating and squab cushions are found throughout the Mediterranean.**

Below **The earthenware plate and jug look as if they are Provençal in design, but they were in fact made by a local potter in Savoie, from where the owner's family comes.**

Thick walls – their stone core clad in *beurrée* mortar – make the house warm in winter and cool in summer.

Although modern houses in Provence are often built to look as though traditional building methods have been used, many of them are made with a concrete core which is then insulated and coated with a mortar-like finish. The old method – the one used here – was to build the walls with a stone core and render the exterior with lime mortar known as *beurrée*. This method ensured thick walls, which meant that the house was cool in summer and warm in winter. The beautiful curved rose and ochre roof tiles are known as *ronde* or *canal* tiles – the shape traditionally supposed to have been formed by being moulded around a woman's thigh; they have been made to the same design and in the same way since the Romans occupied Provence, and they still fulfil their purpose to perfection, being proof against rain, frost and wind – even the mistral.

When the present owner moved in, there were changes to be made, particularly since the house had been empty for a long period. He rationalized the spaces, made chimneys, opened up windows and knocked out unnecessary partitions –

in other words, did just as Provençal dwellers have always done, adapting the original space to a new way of life. There are no really radical changes: the ground-floor living room and kitchen are separate but connected, linked by doors and also a large hatch or window. There are four bedrooms, as well as outbuildings, one of which he has converted into a further bedroom and a garage–woodshed.

The furniture, each piece of which looks as though it has been specially designed for the house, comes in fact from the owner's

family home in Savoie – the mountainous area of eastern France where, as in Provence, there is a traditional, independent way of life; perhaps this is why the furniture seems to fit in so well. In the small garden he has planted trees, including limes (lindens), which traditionally in Provence were planted while a house was being built, so that they would grow as the house aged, giving shade and rest.

The overall effect is one of placid contentment – of a house where peace is easily found and seldom lost.

Above **On one side of the Provençal raised chimney piece in the kitchen are two generous seats covered with a multitude of cushions in ethnic designs.**

Opposite, above left **A small bedroom is decorated in soft terracottas and creams – colours of the countryside that suit the house's mellow style.**

Opposite, right **A dolphin-armed period chair and a rustic Savoie-style armoire are complemented by the colours of the rag rug and bright cushion.**

Opposite, below **On the roof are traditional Provençal tiles, still made by traditional methods.**

Left and inset *Great pains have been taken to deconstruct and reinvent the feel of a medieval village house, but in the hands of the master decorator there is an element of sophistication that makes each room a perfect picture. The walls have been rubbed back to their early plaster and given a distemper wash; the woodwork has been rubbed down and lightly waxed. It is the conjunction of fine pieces of furniture and ceramics set against a background of distressed colour and patina, as well as worn terracotta tiles, that gives each room its charm.*

a house of surprises

This old house in the medieval area of Hyères could be mistaken for a fairytale castle. There is a romance and a magic about each of the rooms, filled as they are with a combination of all that is rare and fine, coupled with the everyday and the practical. Its owner is the celebrated French decorator Frédéric Méchiche.

In many medieval villages of Provence, the houses lining the winding narrow streets are so higgledy-piggledy that they look as if they have been stuck together with a special builder's superglue. They are not particularly large and, being both tall and narrow, many consist of no more than a single room on each floor. Frédéric Méchiche, the well-known French decorator, has for several years owned a house in Hyères that exemplifies the vernacular style: it is tiny with a terracotta and wood staircase that twists upwards, presenting each floor with a flourish as it turns. When he took possession of the house it had not been touched for many, many years and, not surprisingly, everything had to be done. What was surprising was that he decided to do a great deal of it himself. Granted, it is a relatively small space, but, as even the keenest of home restorers knows, even a small space can seem to be a very large space when you are doing it yourself.

Although, in capital cities across the world, Frédéric Méchiche produces for his clients interiors of notable sophistication and

Above and top **In a corner leading off the sitting room is a small dining area that has been simply furnished with a circular table surrounded by folding metal chairs. On an old wooden commode is a rare ceramic charcoal burner dating from the Directoire period. As in the main part of the sitting room, the walls are composed of several** layers of blue, which have been distressed and rubbed to show the variations of colour.

Above right and opposite **This kitchen is not in the main house, but in a smaller guest house across the road. It is decorated but unmodernized. Why not? Everything is to hand, looks charming and works efficiently.**

urbanity, his personal choice – at least, when it comes to a weekend retreat – is pared-down simplicity, with the origins of the house clear for all to see.

Central to this idea was the appearance of the walls; it was important to the decorator that the walls should look distressed, but attractive; that they should show their age and history, but also have some interest and colour. This was not simply a question of cleaning the existing surface. He stripped back the walls, sanding, rubbing, adding a little pigment and polishing until they were at the right stage of layered decay, and until he had the required effect – a surface that was neither new nor old, which both reflected light and acted as a background for whatever he put against it.

Bedrooms and bathrooms are on the lower floors. Halfway up the house, and leading out onto a small balcony, is the living room – an accurate description of such a multipurpose space. The largest part of it is the sitting room, with a small dining area on one side and a small but cleverly equipped kitchen on the other. Within this room, Frédéric has subtly combined the simple

This page and opposite **The mix
of the fine and the rare is shown
to perfection in the sitting room.
Apart from an inviting sofa – its
loose covers made of old linen –
there are a 19th-century French
metal circular table and a 19th-
century cylindrical iron plate
warmer holding a collection of
early earthenware. Above the
sofa, and in contrast to the
roughly painted wooden
cupboard doors, is a small
collection of 18th-century white
porcelain, made in the period
after the deaths of Louis XVI
and Marie-Antoinette. On the
adjoining walls are two ceramic
ovals and a plaster relief.**

and the artisanal with the refined. Against the distressed backdrop – a cross between duck-egg blue and the colour of a cloudy spring sky – are pieces of furniture that, although they date from the 18th and 19th centuries, are neither grand nor courtly. A classical sofa and an 18th-century chair stripped back to the wood – both pieces upholstered with simple cream covers – have been placed in front of an unpainted wooden cupboard used to display delicate 18th-century porcelain. A small dining table is teamed with traditional folding metal chairs, light enough in appearance not to overcrowd the space. An old pot cupboard holds plates and on top is an 18th-century urn.

As well as all these strange and unusual objects and finishes, there is one further surprise in this miniature house of surprises. At the very top of the building, Frédéric Méchiche has created the most perfect of tiny gardens, complete with seating, shade and tubs of odiferous plants. It is the ultimate finishing touch to the place – for him, a very personal project and a very fulfilling one at that.

Left It was this view that first attracted the owners to the location, although the house that stood there was not at all what they desired. Now, several years on, both the view and the house are all that they could want. A covered terrace leading from the kitchen makes an ideal spot for taking in the panorama.

Below and right Rocanour the Jack Russell guards the kitchen, whose doors were painstakingly tracked down by Isabelle. A 17th-century chimney piece has been built in at one side.

Below right The doorways have been arched and old doors installed throughout the house.

a creative triumph

Up in the hills behind Cannes, between Mougins and Grasse, is a summit from which the Mediterranean Sea can be seen, glinting beyond the grey-green of the cypresses and olive groves. This was the spot found by Isabelle and her husband, a place of great beauty – where there was a house of no beauty at all.

All is not what it seems on these pages – indeed, it is the opposite of what it seems. The house illustrated here may look like the archetypal Provençal escape – elegant and solid and constructed between the 17th and 18th centuries – but it is in fact a mid-20th-century house of little merit that has been comprehensively rebuilt, using, as far as the owners were able, not contemporary versions of the old, but authentic and period fixtures and fittings, from the front door to the imposing chimney pieces and even the shutters.

Having discovered some years ago the wonderful hilltop spot behind Cannes, Isabelle and her husband knew that that was where they wanted to be, so they persuaded the owner of the unimpressive house to let it to them, and later to sell it to them, and they lived

Above and opposite **Everything in this living space, from the table and chairs to the beautiful old chimney piece, seems simply to have 'happened'. The pale paving stones, known as** barres de Montpellier, **were found in Apt. Large tubs of dried flowers and other naturally inspired artefacts, from bleached stone balls to a tumbled pile of coral,** make up the decoration and – incongruous but charming – an elaborate, crystal-dropped chandelier lights the scene.

Top and above right **It is hard to believe that nothing is original. From the authentic stone floor to the worn, painted doors and table, every element seems to gleam with the patina of time.**

there with their three young sons for the next seven years. But Isabelle never stopped thinking about how they could have a house that matched the natural beauty of the setting, and as their children grew they began to change the house into their dream dwelling.

You often hear of people who restore a once fine house from ruinous foundations, but it is not so often that you hear of people who decide to turn a 1950s house into one that might have been built 200 years earlier. Perhaps it might have been easier to pull down the original house and start again, but that was not their chosen route. Instead, they moved into a tiny house nearby and, with the help of architect Philippe Caron and a team of specialist craftsmen and builders, began to transform the ugly duckling.

Little by little, Isabelle and her husband ameliorated, extended and improved their residence. Isabelle was determined, really determined, to find the right pieces of the right age, and this she did – even though it took three years of total devotion to her cause. The outer walls were made thicker and were then faced with the

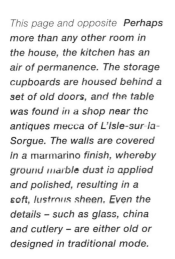

This page and opposite **Perhaps more than any other room in the house, the kitchen has an air of permanence. The storage cupboards are housed behind a set of old doors, and the table was found in a shop near the antiques mecca of L'Isle-sur-la-Sorgue. The walls are covered in a marmarino finish, whereby ground marble dust is applied and polished, resulting in a soft, lustrous sheen. Even the details – such as glass, china and cutlery – are either old or designed in traditional mode.**

particular bleached stone of the area. The doorways and many of the windows were enlarged, the latter acquiring the glazing bars typical of the period as well traditional, softly arched tops, and the façade was graced by a handsome late-18th-century double door found in L'Isle-sur-la-Sorgue.

Inside, the work continued in the same vein. The floors were covered with pale old flagstones, and large antique chimney pieces were hauled into place. Isabelle spent a great deal of time seeking out old building materials, from the functional –

windows, shutters and doors – to the more decorative, such as furniture and accessories, making sure that everything was authentic and would add to the mood and atmosphere of the new–old house. This is where she and her family differed from most restorers, in that most people undertaking a project of this type, although searching out the finishing touches, would be likely to settle for reproduction shutters, doors and so on that merely give the impression of age. Isabelle was anxious to use on walls throughout the house the traditional *marmarino*

This page and opposite **The upstairs rooms are large, open and uncluttered, with a timeless feel. In keeping with tradition, there are relatively few pieces of furniture in each bedroom. Colours are predominantly pale and light, textiles are old, and patterns or designs naturally hark back to the past. Isabelle has acquired several sets of old linen sheets – still relatively easy to find, particularly in the markets of southern France – and has bought old pieces of toile de Jouy to use for covering cushions and for decorative curtain details. The antique cupboard doors harmonize with the rest of the timeless look.**

Walls throughout the house are covered in *marmarino*, a decorative finish that uses polished ground marble dust, giving a wonderful softness and depth.

finish, created by a specialist decorative technique involving polished ground marble dust, which results in a wonderful softness and depth.

Now the rooms are open and spacious, punctuated by antique furniture, as well chosen as everything else. The kitchen, leading out onto a covered terrace – a traditional feature of Provençal houses – is typical. An antique kitchen table, found at a *brocante*, is flanked by a smaller zinc work table and a range of cupboards whose contents are hidden by antique cabinet doors. As was customary in old farmhouses, on one wall is a huge stone hearth and fireplace. The central reception room is airy and cool with stone floors, a fireplace and sofas draped in antique textiles. Bedrooms are equally light and spacious, furnished with simplicity and style.

Although Isabelle wanted the house to exude the air of the 18th century, all the essential underpinnings – heating, bathrooms and kitchen equipment – are as 21st century as could be hoped for, for the whole idea was to make a house that was both delightful and comfortable to live in. Although it is a modern creation – wonderfully conceived, but modern none the less – it both looks and feels genuinely old, too, making it both a creative triumph and a *tour de force*.

Above and right In a corner that catches the evening light is an outdoor dining space that goes beyond a simple terrace and pergola. This is a room without walls, down to the fireplace and chimney along one side, offering both warmth and a heat source for cooking. A terracotta wash over a blue-green base is used to decorate the room; the blue-green colour is picked up by the painted fretwork cornice.

Opposite, above and below Every advantage has been taken of the spacious grounds, which include cool green lawns and a sheltered swimming pool.

Roman inspiration

A low-lying building, shaded by trees, the old *mas* near St Rémy is a quiet and peaceful place. Painted outside in washed-out pink with traditional blue shutters, inside it is decorated with a verve and originality that is very modern, yet based on traditional Provençal colours and patterns.

The city of Glanum, just outside what is now St Rémy, was – between the 1st century BC and the third century AD – a busy Gallo-Roman centre. While little remains today of the ancient city, save a triumphal arch and an impressive mausoleum, the spirit of the Roman colonizers is still alive in St Rémy – and was perhaps the inspiration behind the individual and unusual modern-day stone mosaic floors laid by Bruno

and Hélène Lafforgue in their St Rémy *mas*,
or farmhouse. In several rooms and passages,
they have created concrete floors, either tinted
with pigment or left plain, into which, while the
concrete was wet, they have set pebbles and
stones, arranged into patterns – sometimes
an abstract design, sometimes the curl of a
wave, sometimes a geometric design based
on traditional tile patterns. In the sitting room,

Opposite *A large kitchen that doubles as a winter dining room is furnished and decorated in a way that may appear cluttered but which is in fact carefully worked out. Although many different styles of object are gathered together, there is unity through colour – or lack of it. A flamboyant plaster relief is propped against the chimney, a painted armoire is filled with crockery, and a set of ordinary wooden shelves are made extraordinary by the addition of boughs twisted into a shape that resembles the decorative moulding of a dresser (hutch).*

This page *A white-painted dresser (hutch) is filled with pottery and china in every shade of white and cream. The overall effect is both interesting and restful.*

the squared design of pebbles – with larger pebbles marking the corner of every square – is akin to an old stone and ceramic-tiled floor. Swirls of pebbles set into ochre-tinted concrete greet you on the upper landing, and the bedrooms have their own designs, including, in one bright room, concrete edged with a double row of pebbles, for all the world like a broad-bordered country rug.

Although Provence itself does not exactly lack colour – colour is everywhere you look, from the fields of sunflowers and lavender to the shutters and walls of village houses – it has been used in this house with a particular vivacity. In the living room, which has floor-to-ceiling bookshelves, the walls are painted a clear yellow and the shelves are edged with a scalloped wooden pelmet painted peppermint green, which runs around the top of the wall and across the window. The Lafforgues have a fondness for fretted wood – a slightly sharper version of the pelmet can be seen above another bookcase in the house. There is also one in the outdoor dining room, which is open on three sides, making it a cross between a conventional room and a pergola; the fourth side consists of a bright ochre chimney wall containing a deep fireplace, across the top of which runs the wooden fretwork pelmet. Instead of a roof, the dining space is protected by wooden beams covered not with tiles but panels of split bamboo.

Above and above right **In a small, mainly white bedroom, the floor comes as a subtle surprise. In a base of creamy concrete, a curling pattern of pebbles has been laid, imitating the swirls of an antique rug.**

Opposite, above **Pebbles are set into the floor of another simple bedroom, which is further embellished with exuberantly decorated yellow wooden beds.**

Opposite, below **A sunburst spray of pebbles has been laid to greet those who arrive on the first-floor landing.**

Back in the house, the kitchen, which doubles as a winter dining room, is a nicely haphazard mix of the old, the interesting, the useful and the just plain odd – anything amusing or pretty, as long as it is in white or cream. This gives layers of texture and shape, from the wire-painted armoire full of crocks to the white plaster bas-relief over the fireplace, and the white, floor-length cloth covering the oval table. Two sets of shelves flanking the sink are outlined in bent and twisted twigs, resembling a rococo plaster or carved wood moulding.

There is more white upstairs where, in a bedroom under the eaves, a floor of white concrete reflects the white-painted roof beams and

the white walls; the windows are dressed with white linen, as is the bed; the contrast of textures gives the room both variety and a sense of calm. In striking contrast, in a further bedroom blue and yellow predominate; using paint alone, a dado rail, panels, skirting boards (baseboards) and window surrounds have been created in a cheerful, uplifting combination of colour and pattern.

The house is utterly natural, both in the use of natural artefacts and traditional pigments and in the arrangement and decoration of the various rooms. It is also, perhaps surprisingly, sophisticated, young and rural – a complex combination that is never easy to get right.

romantic

Provence is one of those places where there is little need to search for romance – indeed, one would be hard-pressed, were one to live there, not to be romantic. For a start, there is the romance of the past. In a region inhabited since the Bronze Age, the waves of invaders and settlers, both before and after the Roman conquest, mean that in almost every town and village there is a reminder of what has gone before, sometimes in a name, sometimes in an architectural fragment. And then, too, there is the romance of every day – the easy, relaxed pace of life, the emphasis on the natural, the comfortable, the pleasurable. It is no wonder that so many Provençaux decorate in romantic fashion, choosing the softest of colours and textiles, mixing pattern and design with abandon, and relishing the contrasts of tone and texture inside and outside the home.

Left **In a corner of the kitchen, by a window, is a marble-topped bistro table, used for reading and writing, and paired with a comfortable chair and cushion covered in an old fabric from the owners' collection.**

Above **The owners' collections of ceramics, furniture and textiles – among other things – are put to good use in their country retreat.**

Right **Outside is a dining area in which grows a palm planted by the owners 30 years ago.**

a converted stable

Le Vieux Jas was once a stable – one of the many outbuildings attached to a large *bastide* built in the 18th century by the Marquis d'Espagnet. The *bastide* was designed by the Marquis as a rural retreat within easy reach of the fashionable spa town of Aix-en-Provence.

Founded by the Romans as a hot springs settlement called Aqua Sextiae, Aix was the capital of Provence for 600 years, from the 12th century until the French Revolution, and the town's appearance and ambience today – its houses, wide streets and cosmopolitan and artistic life – reflect its earlier eminence.

One of the most beautiful cities in France, Aix is renowned for its festivals, its café life and its many markets. During the 18th century it became fashionable to have a *maison principal* in Aix, and many aristocrats constructed elegant palaces in the town, such as the Hôtel d'Espagnet, built by the Marquis d'Espagnet on the famous Cours Mirabeau. In common with many of his fellow Aixois, the marquis also built a large *bastide* outside the city. A *bastide* is a classical bourgeois country house – neither a chateau, nor a farmhouse –

Many pieces are family heirlooms, both French and Italian; others have been collected over the years from markets and antique shops throughout France.

sometimes called *une maison de gentilhomme*. It was the *bastide* built by the Marquis d'Espagnet that the current owners found when they first began to look for a house in the region.

'Thirty years ago we left Italy and decided to buy a house near Aix. My husband had family here, and the Aixoise countryside was something he dreamed about during his time in the industrial north of Italy,' explains his wife. Even three decades ago, it was hard to find an old house in this ever-popular area of France, but the family were ready for, and used to, the idea of restoration work. 'It was of course very large, and complete with all the outbuildings, where wine was once made, crops were stored and animals housed.'

Over a period of 30 years, the couple lived in the *bastide* and restored it, but eventually, after their children had grown up, it became too large for their needs, so they turned their attention to the stable.

'It was not a pretty building, and not particularly ornamental,' says one, 'but it was a building of the right proportions, and one to which we felt we could give a new life.' There were inevitable planning constraints, but they were eventually able to start to convert the stable into a house they call 'bourgeois,

Above **Part of the owners' textile collection is used to great effect as curtains and coverings for the antique chairs and stool that they have arranged around a Louis XVI-style fireplace, surmounted by a late 18th-century mirror.**

Top **The unusual and highly dramatic Louis XIII banquette seat has been covered in a later 19th-century deep-red floral toile that perfectly complements the curved lines of the seat itself.**

Opposite **A piece of 18th-century toile peinte, found in a local bastide, is displayed at one end of the airy living room; its colours set the tone for the other textiles used on chairs and tables.**

Left The kitchen has been kept simple – even old-fashioned – in appearance. Appliances and utensils are hidden from view on shelves covered with a small-checked cotton fabric. Colours are calm and peaceful, and it is easy to imagine that the room has been here for 100 years. The hob is set into an old chimney piece, which was found elsewhere and installed in Le Vieux Jas, as was the marble double sink.

Below Part of the owners' ceramic collection is displayed on shelves and walls.

Right An old ironwork panel in the form of a lyre embellishes a window above the sink.

rather than rustic'. Many things were required. Old tiles and reclaimed parquet were found; doors and windows were put in, and made secure with old wrought-iron grilles.

A problem that many house owners face is how best to use pieces of furniture that were originally bought and intended for much larger spaces. In this case, much of the furniture consisted of family items, both French and Italian; other pieces had been collected over the years from markets and antique shops throughout France.

Part of the answer, they decided, was to use the large-scale pieces with confidence. So the principal rooms are filled with groups of tables and chairs, sofas and seats. In one corner, an elegant break-front bureau stands behind a high wing chair covered in bright cherry linen; behind another arrangement of seats is an 18th-century painted toile bought from another *bastide* in the region. The spectacular Louis XIII eight-seater banquette is covered in a 19th-century printed fabric and grounded by a collection of footstools on the floor and an intricate grouping of pictures on the wall behind. The second secret

There are patterns everywhere, but they are restrained and subtle, all working together as part of a larger scheme based on 'unity of colour and textiles'.

ot successful furniture arranging in this family's manner is to tie everything together with what they describe as 'unity of colour and textiles' – blue-reds, pinks, blues, greys and delicate whites. There are many different patterns, but they are restrained and subtle, all working together as part of a larger scheme.

Assembling the textiles was easier for this owner than it would be for many others, since she has over a long period collected them at fairs, second-hand sales and attic sales in the region. 'The armoires are full of them; they are my little reserve of decoration, for one no longer finds them so easily, but at least you can now buy modern re-editions, some of which are very good.'

She has deliberately kept the paint colour pale. 'It was not always fashionable to have strong colour on the walls; I prefer soft whites, and, in any case, I didn't think that matching very strong colour with all those objects and textiles would work.'

The result, at Le Vieux Jas, is a country house for grown-ups – where everything has its place and all is harmony and peace.

Left and above **The air of peace in the upstairs rooms is in part to do with the arrangement of furniture but also with the clever use of textiles and the choice of paint colours – for both furniture and walls. An old armoire has been newly painted, but in the tones of 19th-century furniture.**

Above left **The twin beds have also been painted in soothing tones and the wall-hung corona makes an intriguing centrepiece. Curtains and bed covers are in various shades of white. The central light fitting harmonizes with the drapery on the wall.**

Left and right **The charming garden room was once the space where tractors and other essential pieces of agricultural equipment were kept. Now, transformed by the addition of three tall French windows, it serves in winter as a semi-conservatory and in summer as a dining room for when the sun is too strong for outdoor dining.**

Below and below right **The old farmhouse's pleasing lines will appeal to every lover of rural France. Restoring it meant also giving it back its pride; the façade is a soft limewashed pink with white shutters, and a paved and gravelled terrace runs the length of the house, flanked with square terracotta pots and edged with box.**

perfection in pink

For Enrica Stabile, it was love at first sight. The house at Le Thor was exactly her idea of what a Provençal farmhouse should be: a perfect rectangular shape, with an old well in the front, two large shady plane trees and, on either side of the building, broad fields, bright with poppies and golden sunflowers.

Italian designer Enrica Stabile bought her farmhouse at Le Thor, near Avignon, 12 years ago – at a time 'before Peter Mayle', as she puts it, when prices were much lower. The sundial on an outside wall gives the date of the building as 1870. When she first saw it, it was in a dilapidated state – 'more a ruin than a house' – but she fell in love with it at first sight, and decided to buy it almost immediately, to the bewilderment of her family.

'When I called my family to say that I was buying a house, they thought me completely mad. They said that they would never come, and I would have to do everything myself.' So she did. 'That first year was very difficult. As in many old farmhouses, the animals had been housed downstairs along with the hay and the agricultural machinery. Upstairs had been lived in, but

the disparate items are pulled together by Enrica's colour-filled collections of everything from baskets to ceramics, glass and kitchenware. Under an elaborate chandelier, a large, old trestle table is laid, with traditional garden chairs around it. A further table, this one more workaday, runs parallel to the cooking range and sink.

The kitchen is packed with decorative pieces as well as everything needed for preparing and eating food. It is much lived in – all the family loves to cook.

it was all very primitive. It needed major work. The roof was replaced, the windows repositioned, and, on top of that, I had to make all the bathrooms.'

There is nothing a determined woman in love cannot achieve when she wants to, particularly if, like Enrica Stabile, she is already a successful antique dealer and decorator. The house today is very different from the ruin she first saw. Upstairs there are five bedrooms and three bathrooms. The bedrooms are mainly decorated in a rich buttery colour, the bathrooms in pink: 'It makes you look healthy, especially in the mornings.'

Each bedroom has its own character and colour and is filled with print and pattern used in ingenious and quirky ways. 'I have a passion for textiles. I come from the fashion world, so I love to use and mix them, and create subtle or startling effects according to the room and the season.'

Downstairs, on the ground floor, are a south-facing sitting room, a kitchen–dining room in what was the stables and a small study complete with piano. There is also a wonderful garden room that was once the

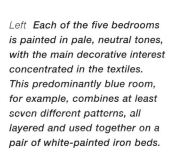

Left **Each of the five bedrooms is painted in pale, neutral tones, with the main decorative interest concentrated in the textiles. This predominantly blue room, for example, combines at least seven different patterns, all layered and used together on a pair of white-painted iron beds.**

Above and right **Red is the main colour in this room, with not only checks of varying sizes but also floral borders and antique red and white cushions. The effect is softened with lush swags of white muslin, draped in deep folds the length of the bed. Muslin curtains hang beneath a soft, scalloped, red and white check pelmet.**

home of tractors and other agricultural essentials, where Enrica installed three tall French windows; now the space is used all year – in winter as a semi-conservatory, sheltering the more delicate plants and the lemon trees from the sometimes cruel weather; and in summer as a shaded dining room when it is too hot to sit outside. As so often in farmhouses, the kitchen, which incorporates a large dining area, is warm and welcoming, coloured in 'a mixture of cream and green with touches of red; it sounds awful but it works.' It is packed

with decorative pieces as well as all the things necessary for cooking and eating. It is much lived in. The whole family, including children and grandchildren, love to cook – and, of course, everyone loves to eat.

The south-facing sitting room is another favourite spot, decorated around a striking pink and blue Murano glass chandelier, given to Enrica by her husband as an olive branch after she went ahead and bought the house. The family's initial disapproval and unwillingness to join in the project has

This page and opposite **The bathrooms, with the exception of one broadly based blue one, are predominantly pink because, in Enrica's opinion, pink makes you look healthy, especially in the mornings. Whether blue or pink, though, her bathrooms are decorated with a judicious mix of the pretty and the practical. The main features are large, old baths and basins – she prefers never to buy new, although she has made a concession to her plumber with the lavatories and bidets. There are also various decorative plates on the walls, embroidered antique towels and antique mirrors and lights. As elsewhere in the house, there are flower-filled glasses and jugs everywhere you look.**

'I just bought little by little through the years – a few good pieces and many nice inexpensive things to make the house really warm and welcoming.'

dispersed but, as Enrica remarks, 'Now the house is beautiful and comfortable, they all adore it and come – and even help in the garden. As I remind them, they are very welcome but they are just my beloved guests.'

Enrica understands the art of arrangement, and each corner holds a combination of objects, flowers and furniture. 'As far as furniture goes, I was lucky because I didn't have anything apart from some nice things my husband gave me from a former family house, so I just bought little by little through the years. I bought a few good pieces and many nice inexpensive things to make the house really warm and welcoming, as I spend as much time as I can here. I have never actually bought anything new, except the bidet and lavatory – so as not to disappoint my plumber completely.'

And now that the house is finished? 'I'm an antique dealer and a designer, so it has been a most rewarding job to do my own house in the way I liked best. Now that it's over, I feel pretty desperate and need a new challenge.' Given Enrica's determination and style, that challenge surely cannot be long in coming.

Left and right **Every part of this old stone house is used as living space. Here, in the shade of the original stone steps that lead to the upper part of the house, Diana has carved out a seating and eating area, overhung with wisteria trained along a pergola. A rustic table made from blocks of stone and a low wall, turned** into an inviting bench with the addition of faded blue cushions, provides a perfect place to sit shaded from the midday sun.

Below and below right **The kitchen is a comfortable and familiar room, incorporating pine cupboards and traditional Provençal-print curtains.**

pretty as a picture

Diana Bauer and her husband found their 300-year-old farmhouse in Cotignac 45 years ago, long before the current wave of Provence-lovers descended on the region. When they bought the house, it was tiny, and almost a ruin, not having been lived in for 50 years.

Cotignac is one of the prettiest of the Haut-Var villages that perch high above the Mediterranean in a region dominated by vineyards and olive and chestnut groves. Like most other villages in the area, it is not a summer-only place. Go there in midwinter or spring and you will find open shops and cafés, competitive boules games in progress and a thriving weekly market.

When the Bauers bought the house, it consisted of just a downstairs living room with a sleeping alcove in the wall, an upstairs room for storing hay and an outbuilding used as a stable. Since it hadn't been lived in for a very long time, much had to be done to make it habitable without destroying the sense and charm of the original building. The first task was to deal with the structure – in particular, to renovate the stonework,

Below In keeping with the rest of the house, the main bedroom is, above all, comfortable. Two chairs – one a traditional French rocking chair, the other an old French country chair – are both conducive to relaxation.

Right A sleeping alcove in the living room has become a real hideaway – ideal for relaxing close to the fire on a winter's evening, and equally convenient as an extra bed space.

Opposite Architecture has been put to good use in another part of the garden, where a low wall doubles as a bench in front of a table. Set underneath a fig tree, the scene is illuminated by an appropriate flowerpot light.

There was originally just a downstairs living room with a sleeping alcove in the wall, an upstairs room for storing hay and an outbuilding used as a stable.

which had deteriorated badly over the years. The next project was to add an internal staircase; at that time the only way to reach the upper rooms was by external stone steps. To retain the sense and manner of the original, the Bauers made the ground floor into a living space and kitchen, and converted the old hay loft into two large and one small bedrooms and a bathroom.

The sleeping alcove in the downstairs room was made into a whitewashed, cushion-piled bed to be used day and night. In the kitchen, too, all has been done with the utmost simplicity. There are pine doors under the worktops and a large pine cupboard used as a larder. Upstairs bedrooms have old terracotta floors, simple furniture, rag rugs and American patchwork quilts, which work very well in these light-filled rooms.

In the garden, several large pieces of stone topped with a rough-hewn slab were used to make a table in front of a stone bench which protrudes from the walls of the house; elsewhere, a low wall doubles as a bench. French windows curve round the house, making inside and out appear as one. The original outside staircase is flanked with pots of geraniums and lavender, and vines and wisteria climb over the terrace. It is unpretentious and charming and completely of Provence.

This page and opposite **In a large 19th-century village house, typical of many still to be found in every region of France, Carole Ouhlen has restored the space to something of its former grandeur. In what was the only major structural alteration, a large kitchen and dining room has been made downstairs from what was once an outhouse that served as a garage. It now is a light, sunny room leading onto a broad terrace and from there to the garden. It has been decorated with taste and restraint. The colours are pale, the furniture carefully chosen and the details – the lined baskets beneath the sink mirrored by more baskets above the armoire – are in keeping with the overall style of the house.**

lyrical legacy

Carole Ouhlen lives with her husband and children in a large, early 19th-century house in a village outside Avignon. Neither a *mas* nor a *manoir*, it is the sort of house that can be seen in villages across France: solid, well built, and with a personality – and a history – very much its own.

Once a silkwork farm, the house was also, in the 19th century, the home of one of the poets who belonged to the Félibrige, a literary society whose members included Frédéric Mistral, Provence's most famous poet, and whose aim was to restore Occitan, *la langue d'Oc*, the old language of Provence.

Carole bought the house two years ago and, although she appreciated its turn-of-the-century past, she wanted to adapt it for a modern family. Much structural work was needed, so that by the time she came to what most people think the most interesting and amusing task – the furnishing and decorating of the rooms – her budget was limited. If anything, the house has benefited from the discipline. In every room, clean lines dominate; colours are gentle, furnishings are restrained. The impression is one of open simplicity. For example, the hall is

Natural fabrics such as linen and muslin predominate, in soft stone shades or traditional patterns such as two-toned toiles de Jouy and old floral designs.

distinguished by fine 19th-century encaustic floor tiles, an integral part of the house which Carole has made into a prominent feature. She has surrounded the tiles with shades of stone – pale walls with bands of deeper colour – so that the hall makes a decorative statement that attracts the eye towards the other rooms.

Leading off the hall are the living room and the large kitchen and dining room. When the Ouhlens bought the house, attached to it was a large outhouse used as a garage. They decided to knock through from the house into the garage to make one large space, now a combined kitchen and dining room, opening directly onto a terrace and the garden. It is a fine room, simply furnished and coloured, with clever touches such as baskets of differing sizes beneath the sink to hide unattractive essentials, and a large painted armoire whose panels are filled with metal mosquito screening instead of glass.

The kitchen was the only room that was changed structurally. The configuration of the other rooms remains the same. The large living

Above left and above **The large living room leads off the original entrance hall and is decorated, like the rest of the house, in calm, pale colours.**

Opposite, above left and right **The furniture too is neither all old nor all new; rather, each piece is chosen for its place in the finished picture.**

Right **Pale linens and cottons are Carole's first choice, but she also likes the soft patterns of traditional toiles de Jouy.**

Far right **The entrance hall, with its distinctive encaustic tiles, is a decorative feature in itself, with bands of painted colour in varying shades of stone.**

room is furnished as straightforwardly as the kitchen – a room of calm and peaceful colours emanating from Carole's favourite palette of stone shades. There are three bedrooms upstairs and one downstairs.

The furniture incorporates a mixture of styles, with pieces chosen for their design and charm rather than rarity, and often painted in soft shades by Carole, who is an artist at heart. The textiles follow the same path – natural fabrics such as linen and muslin with accents of colour in the fabrics used for cushions and throws, and traditional patterns such as two-toned toiles de Jouy and old floral designs.

Once a deep burgundy, the façade of the house is now an ochre-yellow. Its garden owes much to the design of the early 19th century, with such charming features as old walls, a pond and old fruit trees. The whole ensemble seems perfect – perhaps because Carole is a perfectionist. She is also someone who loves to restore old houses, and it would be no surprise if another sleeping house soon finds itself shaken awake by this restorer of sensitivity and taste.

Opposite **In the main bathroom, which is en suite, Carole has cleverly converted an antique washstand into an up-to-date, plumbed unit. The new ceramic basin, reminiscent of an antique china bowl, and the marble-topped, painted wooden stand look as if they have always been there; only the wall-hung taps (faucets) give the secret away.**

Above **In another bathroom, a similar effect of permanence has been achieved by the installation of a free-standing rolltop bath, a ladder-style rail and a crystal-drop chandelier.**

Above left and top **Pale, limpid tones and neutral fabrics make for bedrooms that are both cool and restrained.**

classical restoration

Like so many other country houses – particularly in the large rural areas of France – the fortunes of this recently renovated *bastide* took a turn for the worse in the 19th century, when it slowly degenerated from elegant 18th-century mansion into lowly farm, and the gardens were levelled and made into fields.

There is a particular kind of classical French country house that exudes tranquillity and calm – a house that has apparently stood unaltered for many years or even centuries, settled and secure in its own surroundings.

This is the impression given by the Delaune family's *bastide* outside Aix-en-Provence: a fairytale mansion complete with hipped tower, immaculate gardens, an ornamental potager, a real swan lake, and numerous beautiful trees, all apparently cared for by generations of talented gardeners. Inside, large cool rooms, softly coloured walls and comfortable antique furniture on floors of ancient terracotta tiles glowing with the patina of years – all speak of a life of unbroken harmony.

The reality is different. When Christian and Martine Delaune bought the *bastide* in 1999, they acquired

Opposite The painted dining table at one end of the kitchen, designed and made by Daisy Simon, works well with the early 20th-century painted chairs. The tall French windows open onto a vegetable garden, one of the areas that Christian Delaune has painstakingly restored.

Left The drawing room is yet another achievement, seemingly imbued with the permanence of age, but in fact made from what had been a warren of partition-walled spaces, false ceilings and bricked-up windows.

Below The discipline and purity of line that underwrites the Delaune decorating style can be seen to detailed effect in this composition of painted side table and mirror, where every object has been picked for its part in the greater whole.

The result of the Delaunes' restoration work is a triumph. Every room displays a blend of classic design, highlighted with objects of interest and charm.

a ruined farm with small, partition-walled rooms, false ceilings and crumbling beams, flanked by untended fields and pasture. Its attractions included its size – lots of space in which to bring up their four young children – and its abundance of land; also, to their delight, there were several mature trees surviving in what remained of the gardens. Although the house was in a state of bad disrepair when the Delaunes found it, its history was one of vibrant life. Built in the 18th century, it had once been a grand house, with elaborately frescoed ceilings and even more elaborately planted gardens.

The couple had searched for two years before finding their crumbling manor; in that time, Martine collected decorative ideas from books and magazines, so that, when they eventually bought the house, she had a good idea of how she wanted it to look. After removing the partition walls, false ceilings and other 20th-century additions, they set about returning the house as nearly as possible to its original design and architecture.

Fireplaces had been closed up, windows altered, the layout of rooms changed, and, with little archival information, Christian and Martine had to rely to a degree on intelligent guesswork. It took 12 months to

This page and opposite **One of the pleasures of the restoration is the way in which the owners have retained the 'imperfect' structure of the original house and combined it with modern stylishness. Upstairs, for example, they have used such integral elements as the uneven and beautiful old terracotta floor tiles and the heavy ceiling beams as a background to their subtle and delicate brand of interior decoration, where beds are made with pristine white linen, draped with filmy fabric and painted in off-white neutral colours. The result, in both the bedrooms and bathrooms, is a natural and gentle effect that is also remarkably individual and surprisingly practical.**

restore the house – a short enough time, you might think, but at certain periods there were as many as 70 workers on site at the same time.

When the Delaunes had almost finished reviving the heart of the house, they brought in interior decorator Daisy Simon, based in Aix, to help them to find the right furniture and fittings for the place. With her, they travelled around Provence visiting *brocantes* and towns such as L'Isle-sur-la-Sorgue and Aix itself, until they had found enough distinctive pieces for every room.

It was important that their finds should be elegant but not over-elaborate, since the Delaunes had taken care to retain the spirit of the original architecture. The floors of hexagonal terracotta tiles remained uneven, the walls retained their rough texture and were painted – both exterior and interior – with limewash, as would have traditionally been done. As seen on these pages, the result of the restoration is a triumph: a house that really does now exude peace and calm – even if it has only been that way for just over five years.

Left A 19th-century white wrought-iron bed is matched with an unusual 18th-century Swedish commode and, above it, an elegant gilded mirror.

Right and far right In another bedroom is a traditional French colonial iron bed, dating from the 19th century, complete with a curved metal frame; delicate, unlined white curtains are tied in knots along its length. Cushions are made from old pieces of French toile, part of the Hills' collection of textiles. At one side of the room is an imposing 18th-century Swedish painted buffet à deux corps.

Below Dating from the late 18th century, this chair, piled with more toile-covered cushions, still has its original rush seat.

on the ramparts

Light-filled, calm, gentle: soothing adjectives all – and all of which accurately describe the home of the Hill family, built on the ramparts of old Mougins, in the hills behind Nice. 'The ramparts are circular, as befits a fortified village,' says Douglas Hill, 'so our house is actually curved, following the lie of the wall.'

Douglas and Jean Hill, English owners of an antique shop in Mougins called French Country Living, bought a house in the village 12 years ago. Since then, they and their two daughters have transformed the interior so that it has as much charm as the ancient exterior.

When the family found the house, having looked in the area for many years, it had had the same owner for four decades. Decorated in the 1950s, it was clearly in

need of change. Although they knew that much work would have to be done, in the event they had to do far more than they had imagined.

After the restoration had begun, the Hills found out that the roof terrace, erected many years earlier, had pushed the house downwards and outwards – to such an extent that the entire house needed underpinning. 'Every floor had to come down, and the whole house

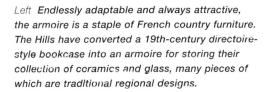

Left **Endlessly adaptable and always attractive, the armoire is a staple of French country furniture. The Hills have converted a 19th-century directoire-style bookcase into an armoire for storing their collection of ceramics and glass, many pieces of which are traditional regional designs.**

Right **A 19th-century armoire, fitted with glazed panels rather than chicken wire or fabric, is used to store large dishes and pots, bottles and jars.**

Above **Other original pieces include this forged-iron painted bench from the 19th century, with cushions made from old blue and white textiles.**

was reinstated using concrete and steel,' says Douglas. This drastic rebuilding had its compensations. 'When the house was gutted, we could appreciate the essential simplicity of the space – especially since, in its former incarnation, one room was bright blue and another bright green. The builders carried out a great feat of engineering. When it comes, the rain here is horizontal, and we've never had a drop inside.' The work took 18 months, and the result was just what they wanted, a house that is very much of the South of France – neither glittery nor flashy, but imbued with the spirit of the area.

After the dramatic house surgery, very little of the original fabric remained, with the exception of some ceiling beams, but the Hills were anxious to achieve a sense of unity. 'I think that

in this type and age of house, you don't dictate to the house – the house dictates to you,' says Douglas. 'It'll tell you what to do, such as having simple flooring, for example.'

Their simple flooring, seen throughout the house, is all one design, of reclaimed hexagonal terracotta tiles, and they also opted for simple wall treatments. 'There is not a straight wall in the house. The plasterwork followed the stone walls, which are themselves curved,' explains Douglas. 'The wall surface is far from smooth. The traditional method is to attach chicken wire to the stone before plastering so that the plaster adheres to the wire rather than slipping off the stone. It's a completely different technique and gives a completely different texture.' When it came to choosing the colour for the walls, the clarity

Above **The house abounds with beautiful painted furniture. This northern Italian 18th-century armoire differs from similar northern European pieces in the amount of decoration imposed on the doors and sides.**

Above right **In the drawing room a late 18th-century pier mirror, inset into a carved and gilded** boiserie **panel, surmounts a decorated 18th-century Italian console table.**

Right and far right **On one side of the English Chesterfield sofa (piled with cushions made from the monogrammed panels of old linen sheets) is a fine Louis XIV bookcase, replete with more carving and subtle decoration.**

of the light in this part of the country determined the colours that the Hills decided to use – such as all the varying soft shades of ochre, which they built up in layers.

As for furnishing this singular house, the Hills indulged their love of 18th-century pieces. 'We like a mixture of French and Italian, which is appropriate to this part of France, and we also like a mixture of painted furniture and fruitwoods – each style helps the other.' There is but one piece of English furniture in the house – an early Chesterfield, which sits happily beside its more southerly neighbours. The whole family loves old textures and textiles. 'Whenever we can, we cover our chairs with old linen that we sometimes dye; we like to mix patterns as well – stripes and checks, toiles and some floral designs.'

From the windows the Hills can see the green slopes of Cap Ferrat and the Mediterranean beyond – a pleasure at any time of year. 'Every day we marvel at the Provençal light, which affects everything down here. We love our house, and know how lucky we are to be here.'

On the book spines:
THE STORY OF CARPETS
ORIENTAL RUGS
ANTIQUAIRES
FRENCH FLOWER PAINTERS
Tuscany Interiors
DECORATIVE ARTS
IN EUROPE 1790-1850
IDENTIFYING MARBLE
GREAT INTERIORS
THE EIGHTEENTH CENTURY
GIORGIO ARMANI
INVESTING IN
GREAT

elegant

Elegance, in whatever sphere, is international. Just as an elegant woman is recognized as such from Buenos Aires to Biarritz, so elegant interior decoration, wherever employed, is seen to make use of the same group of basic, understood elements. There are regional and individual differences, as well as different interpretations, but one thing is certain: there is no elegance without simplicity, for elaboration and ornamentation can never be part of the elegant vocabulary. To utilize this vocabulary in a part of the world where the weather can often be very warm is an additional discipline. In Provence, for example, elegance is a question of using the native style and refining it, taking the best of what is there: a pale painted armoire, a traditional wooden *radassié*, placed in a calm and cool environment, highlighted as objects of beauty in their own right, and surrounded by soft colours and generally muted patterns — all adding up to a look that is classical, but never dull. That is elegance, Provençal style.

Far left *If a sea view through a grove of umbrella pines is your idea of a true Provençal retreat, then nothing could be more perfect than the Villa Marie. Set on a hill above St Tropez, this old farmhouse, now a hotel, has been completely restored, while the land surrounding it has been transformed from scrub into a paradise of cypress and citrus, jasmine and roses.*

Left *The gardens are linked to the interior by airy corridors and hallways, furnished with pieces that work both inside and out.*

decorative delight

When Jocelyne and Jean-Louis Sibuet saw the location of what is now the Villa Marie – on a sloping hill outside the village of Ramatuelle, with views across vineyards to one side and down to the Mediterranean on the other – they could not resist the opportunity to bring yet another old building back to life.

Jocelyne and Jean-Louis Sibuet are from France's Savoie region – a part of the country that has much in common with rural Provence, especially in the appreciation and understanding of artisanal skills and objects. The Sibuets still live in the Savoie – in Megève – and it was there where they first channelled their talents into transforming old, vernacular buildings into small hotels of charm and great individuality.

They began with a mountain lodge, Au Coin du Feu, followed by Les Fermes de Marie, where they turned several rebuilt farmhouses into a small *hameau* of comfort and delight. After more restorations in Megève, the Sibuets ventured further afield, first to Lyons, where they transformed four 15th- and 16th-century town houses into La Cour des Loges, and then south to Provence, where they bought an old farmhouse in the Luberon and made it into La Bastide de Marie.

Unsurprisingly, Provence exerted its powerful allure on the Sibuets and, although they were not originally looking for anywhere on the coast, when they saw the location of what is now the Villa Marie, they could not resist the temptation to embark on a new adventure. What

The rural landscape, which is planted with more than 3,000 new plants and trees, is crowned with a swimming pool that was carved out of the piny, rocky ground around the house and now seems part of the natural terrain.

is unusual, if not exceptional, about the Sibuets is that, although the Villa Marie is their seventh project, every hotel that they have done has the feel of a private house – a large house, to be sure, but a house and a home nevertheless. This is not accidental, but a considered strategy: 'I treat each new hotel exactly as if it were my own second home,' says Jocelyne.

It is also due in large part to the fact that the pair's talents complement each other in a remarkable and highly felicitous way. Jean-Louis is master of the broad brushstroke – the buildings, the landscape – while Jocelyne is queen of the finer details – the colours, the textiles, the look of the thing. They are both interested in old furniture. A decorator and a designer with an interest in common make the perfect match.

The initial plan was to renovate the old building as well as to add new buildings to accommodate a bar, restaurants and a spa, which would come under the umbrella of the original building; they would also landscape the terrain and build a swimming pool that was outstanding and yet in keeping with the setting.

Colour and colouring both inside and out were all-important. In this part of Provence, the colours are drained by the deep, strong light as well as by the reflection of the blue sea and sky. This means that,

This page **Archways and open doors lead the eyes – and the feet – into the gardens, and to the views of the landscape beyond.**

Opposite **Even the swimming pool seems to have happened almost by chance. It has been designed to incorporate a stony outcrop, which becomes an integral part of the pool itself. On one side, a waterfall tumbles into the water; on the other, a wooden deck has been erected that faces down to the sea. Neighbouring pines and the clumps of wild rosemary and thyme scent the air around.**

Right **Shells and other natural finds are an integral part of the interior decoration at Villa Marie, which delights in creating compositions on every available surface. Here, an ornate carved wooden table is used to display a collection of antique candle holders, combined with domed glass jars filled with shells, a stone urn overflowing with ivy and a pair of ceramic doves.**

Far right **Standing on an old terracotta floor in the hallway is another imposing wooden console table, flanked by a pair of antique chairs. It is used to display a collection of shells, driftwood and bleached coral.**

to be successful, colour schemes should either be in calm and pale, neutral-based tones or in shades that can stand up to the natural competition without leaving an impression of clashing tumult.

The Sibuets have solved the problem by embracing both alternatives. The façade is deep ochre, with a traditional terracotta-tiled roof; inside, some equally strong colours can be found, but they relate closely to the Mediterranean area – ochre, sienna and terracotta, but used in conjunction with cool neutral shades such as stone, cream and whites, and also in partnership with some surprising and unusual combinations, sometimes astringent and sometimes warm – colours such as rose, mauve and a soft cool green.

These latter colours are not normally found in this part of the world, nor are they colours that normally grace hotel rooms, no matter how personal the touch; but Jocelyne Sibuet is a natural decorator, and she has the natural decorator's gift of mixing the unusual to produce something new and totally fresh. There are

around 40 bedrooms at Villa Marie and each one has been decorated in its own, highly individual way. Furniture is as important a part of the decorative scheme as the chosen colours, and neither Jocelyne nor Jean-Louis would ever go down the 'contract hotel' route. They love old furniture – Jean-Louis, in particular, has always collected old pieces, both French and Italian, and for Villa Marie they found any number of Provençal pieces, both painted and made in fruitwood, to which they have added decorative bits found in local *brocantes* as well as a few contemporary items to make a thoroughly original

mélange. The finds are scattered through the building accentuated with a collection of natural and sometimes eccentric objects: on an ornate table in a hallway, coral and seashells are arranged as sculptural forms, and around the bar are hundreds of seashells glued into place by Jean-Louis in an arrangement that is both charming and evocative of an earlier era in the French Riviera fable.

The bedrooms are simple in concept, featuring beamed ceilings and artisan-made wrought-iron bedsteads, with the clever colour combinations of walls and furnishings keeping the space cool while

This page and opposite **Each bedroom is decorated in a completely contemporary way, incorporating a mix of antique furniture and modern decorative objects and textiles. Colour schemes are based on the Provençal palette but softened. In this room, the soft bleached green of the summer is paired with a deep purple, the latter** **shade apparent in the carefully delineated flower motif that can be seen on curtains and cushions. The stone urns – a recurring theme throughout the house – here serve as bedside lights and, as elsewhere at Villa Marie, the outdoor world is not far away. Through French windows an iron-balustraded terrace beckons.**

reflecting the light and scents of Provence. Bathrooms open directly off the bedrooms or are located inside the bedrooms themselves. As elsewhere in the hotel, natural fabrics reign supreme – curtains and cushions are in linen, silk or cotton, sometimes striped, sometimes plain, and never too formal or intrusive.

The garden, once scrubland, has been tamed by Jean-Louis Sibuet to make the perfect, rambling Mediterranean garden, with pathways that curl through the pine trees, and the whole area is newly planted with more than 3,000 new plants and trees from palms and cypress to tamarisk and lavender. This rural landscape is crowned with a swimming pool that was carved out of the piny, rocky ground around the house and now seems to be part of the natural terrain.

The whole effect conveyed by Villa Marie is one of careless ease – a testament, perhaps, to the theory that the more effort you put into a project the more effortless it will appear to others.

Right and far right **Unlined linen adorns the bed in this simple bedroom. At the window, which leads onto an ochre-painted balcony, the curtains are a soft honey and white – colours taken from the Provençal countryside.**

Below and below right **Design of the bathrooms is an important** part of the overall concept at Villa Marie, and many are within the bedrooms themselves – placed not at the far side of the room, but near the entrance. Here a freestanding rolltop bath is flanked by a pair of bowl-shaped basins, which look almost as if they have been carved from the rock outside.

Below From the outside, the farmhouse looks as though the years have passed it by. In fact, after a long period of neglect, it has now been heavily restored, including the incorporation of outbuildings into the principal structure. Today it is a light and comfortable house, and one that is entirely of its time.

Right and far right The kitchen, formerly a barn, is today an admirable combination of the efficient and the attractive. The worktop and the tiles behind the range are made from reclaimed black granite, brought from Belgium; the chairs and marble-topped table are both French, and date from the 1940s.

attention to detail

The house featured on these pages, located not far from the town of St Rémy, was not – unlike so many others in the book – searched for over many years or suddenly discovered by happy chance. It was, in fact, the house at the bottom of the garden.

The garden surrounding the St Rémy house belonged to the owner of the property next door, who was, as it happened, very happy with what he already had. But the house had for many years been owned by an elderly couple; after they died, it became apparent that it might be sold and the land developed. Troubled by such a prospect, the next-door neighbour bought the property; only later did he realize that he had acquired a very pleasant space, which could be transformed into something extremely desirable.

What he did not want was a Provençal pastiche or an ersatz farmhouse; it was to be of the area and appropriately rural – reflecting its surroundings, but 'a proper house', sophisticated in tone, with style, and possessing all the necessary technological amenities. It was important, as the owner said, 'Not to be living in someone else's footprints.'

American decorator Kenyon Kramer (see pages 174–81) was asked to help solve the problem, and the decision was taken to rethink the space completely

Left and far left **The decorator Kenyon Kramer has completely remade the house, down to details such as the purpose-built kitchen cupboard, made to a 17th-century design to hold the owner's collection of glazed Moroccan terracotta, as well as linen and other essentials.**

Opposite **As with the worktops in the kitchen, the downstairs flooring consists throughout of reclaimed black granite.**

Below **There is direct access from the dining area to a sunny terrace shaded by giant terracotta-coloured umbrellas.**

and make an interior appropriate for the 21st century. Today, although the house has the appearance from the outside of a sleepy old farmhouse, untouched for many centuries, all is changed. Even the seemingly old, soft-coloured exterior was in fact reclad in local stone, and assembled in dry-point, using a 17th-century method of stonemasonry.

Inside, the only original space is the hallway; the rest has been reconfigured and altered, incorporating some existing outbuildings to create comfortable spaces downstairs, including a vast airy living room, complete with a 17th-century Provençal stone fire surround, and a large kitchen, created from what was once a barn.

Upstairs, the bedrooms are small – deliberately so, with an intimate air – and the witty bathrooms include one that houses a bath transformed out of an old water trough and a basin made from local marble.

Anxious to marry the new and the old, Kramer and his partner, Jean-Louis Raynaud, went to enormous lengths to find appropriate and often original materials for the work of reconstruction. Hence, throughout the upper floor, the floorboards are made from reclaimed oak, discovered in 19th-century railway carriages; on the ceilings, the structural horizontal beams are

There is no clash between the old and the new – the fact that all materials are natural means that there is a blending of styles that work easily together.

original, while the vertical beams are reclaimed. The ceilings themselves have been designed and made in traditional Provençal 18th-century fashion with exposed terracotta tiles – all old, reclaimed ones – visible between the beams.

This same attention to detail is evident in the carpentry and hardware. The cabinets throughout the house imitate rural 17th-century designs, using bleached oak – the wood that would have been used originally – and all the window frames and door frames as well as the door furniture were copied

from traditional models and made by local craftspeople. But not all the materials used are completely traditional: in a bold move, and in strong contrast to the wooden floors upstairs, the flooring throughout the ground floor is reclaimed black granite slabs, brought from Belgium. Interestingly, there is no clash between the old and the new – the fact that all materials are natural means that there is a blending and merging of styles that work easily together. The main living room, made larger by incorporating an outside storage area, is a wonderful

This page and opposite **Holding centre stage in the handsome, well-proportioned living room is an oversized double banquette upholstered in a striking red knot design, which is repeated in the floor-length curtains. Many of the cushions have the same colourway but feature an exuberant floral motif. The fireplace is Provençal, dating from the 17th century. The furniture is a combination of comfortable easy chairs and an unusual collection of French Arts and Crafts pieces, which sit very well in their new rural surroundings.**

space, dominated by a huge double banquette seat, piled with overstuffed cushions. Again, in surprising contrast to both this and the striped armchair, much of the remainder of the furniture is French Arts and Crafts dating from the end of the 19th century. This was chosen deliberately as an answer to the knotty problem of style. The last thing the owner wanted was old painted country furniture, yet smart, sophisticated city furniture or ornamental antiques would not look right in the house either. So the decision was taken to use French Arts and Crafts pieces; these designs retain a hand-made quality and, while looking contemporary, are simple enough in style to work in a country house.

Jean-Louis Raynaud – 'a genius with fabric', says Kenyon – has chosen striking, dominating designs in the sitting room for both furnishings and curtains but has cleverly kept the number of colours used to a minimum – warm terracotta and cream, fading to paler terracotta in the striped chair.

The garden has been kept simple. A pool has been installed, in the shape of a natural pond; an olive grove and an orchard have been planted. It is all very Provençal, and all very simple – just what any lucky person might like to see at the bottom of their garden.

Above **The large structural beams in the upstairs rooms are original; the smaller beams are made from reclaimed wood. In between the beams, the ceiling is set with exposed terracotta tiles in the traditional manner, with air pockets between them and the outer roof tiles. All the upstairs floors are made from reclaimed oak.**

Above right **The bathrooms have a comfortably eccentric air. This bath is a reclaimed water trough carved from a single block of acacia wood; the basin is made from the local marble.**

Opposite **The bedrooms are simple and comfortable, with unlined linen curtains and rugs woven in Morocco.**

rediscovered glory

After she and her husband bought the Chateau de Gignac in 1989, Michelle Joubert took on the task of returning it to the glory it might have enjoyed had not the hand of history intervened; for 16 years, she has been working on the house using only old materials and recreating every room to perfection.

France's size and its turbulent past mean that, particularly in the South, visual reminders of its history are often seen. There is still evidence of the destruction wrought by the 16th-century Wars of Religion, and people tend to talk about the years of the French Revolution as if they had only just taken place.

Take the troubled and, until now, tragic story of the Chateau de Gignac, for example. On the place on which the present chateau stands, there was once a medieval castle. Like many other buildings in the area, this was destroyed during the Wars of Religion. By the 18th century, a new chateau was under construction on the site, built by an old Provençal family, the de Thomas, but just before its completion the events set in train by the French Revolution caused the Marquis de Thomas to flee, never to return, and the chateau, like so many others, fell into disrepair, remaining in that state until the end of the 1980s, when it was bought by François and Michelle Joubert.

Many chateaux in rural France are less like castles than large, sometimes fortified, manor houses; they are often the centre of an agricultural smallholding, and the hub of a community. Looking at Chateau de Gignac today, you can see how, under Michelle Joubert's sensitive direction, such a house would have developed had it been constantly inhabited since the 18th century. Yet there was literally nothing there when the Jouberts bought it; all had to be found and bought – as Michelle says, 'everything, piece by piece' – at auction, in antique shops, at flea markets and *brocantes* and of course in the market of L'Isle-sur-la-Sorgue. Even the bathrooms have been carefully designed to look as though they might have been added at the end of the 19th century rather than at the end of the 20th century.

Although there is this sense of age, and although Michelle Joubert has consistently used old materials, furniture and furnishings, and even though both architecture and decoration consistently refer to the past, the house looks neither old-fashioned nor preserved in amber; indeed, one of its abiding triumphs is that it looks so of the moment –

Left and far left **In part of what
was once the scullery of
Chateau de Gignac, Michelle
has put together a large
collection of Provençal pottery –
all practical, working pieces that
would have been used as often
200 years ago as they are today.
The various pieces are all
displayed and stored in rows
and piles, much as they would
originally have been, and their
glazes, set against a backdrop
of old terracotta and stone, are
seen to antique advantage.**

but a moment achieved with old pieces. In every room, the old is placed in such a way that it looks completely modern, and things that are intrinsically old – textiles, decorative objects and so on, are placed and arranged in a subtle manner. The hall, for example – a dramatic space in any large house – has few pieces of furniture: a flamboyant console table, a large wall-hung mirror and, on the floor, an oversized candlestick; in the curve of the stairwell, sits a traditional Provençal *radassié*, a wood-backed banquette. The relative sparseness of the room serves to emphasize both the sweeping staircase itself and the dramatic cobbled floor, worn in places and evocative of times past.

The same feeling continues throughout the house: the kitchen is a combination of the romantic – an old refectory table and a worn, well-used butcher's block – and the practical, represented by a new cooking range, designed in traditional style and set into the old hearth. The main reception rooms are simple but elegant – moulded plaster panels, carefully chosen pieces of furniture and full curtains that brush the floor.

Opposite **In an upper hall, pale grey walls are emphasized by a deeper dove grey in the alcoves and on the door panels. The original plaster moulding has been restored and painted a soft creamy-white, offsetting the grey and white marble floor tiles.**

This page **Bedroom colours are typically soft and 18th century** in feel. A serpentine commode with marble top is painted in a traditional soft blue, and in a bed alcove the walls are a very pale duck-egg blue, contrasting with, and yet complementing, the soft grey of the rest of the room. The stucco has been left unrestored, and the polished terracotta tiles throw the whole scheme into relief.

The eight bedrooms are reassuringly old-fashioned and yet not fussy; as In the downstairs rooms, there is an air of modern thinking in the way that relatively little furniture Is used in each room, accompanied by only the odd decorative piece. The wall colourings are used to add extra decoration, all silvery and soft: light grey, eggshell blue and pale rose, sometimes contrasting with delicate plaster moulding, and woodwork highlighted in soft French whites.

The bathroom fixtures, traditional in design, are cleverly combined with freestanding pieces of furniture, some originally made to hold washbowls and ewers. Michelle has deliberately decorated the bathrooms with pictures, mirrors and objects more often seen in grander surroundings.

Outside, the gardens and terraces are planted in traditional and Provençal style, with a swimming pool designed in the shape of a long, classical, stone-edged canal. The 18th-century Marquis de Thomas would doubtless have much appreciated the 21st-century Chateau de Gignac.

Above left and opposite **The simply arranged bathrooms are given an air of permanence by a combination of old furniture and new plumbing. In one room, a long piece of furniture, possibly an old dresser (hutch) base, has been converted into a modern basin unit, complete with more than enough storage space for towels and bathroom pieces.**

Top and above **These bedrooms are enlivened with just a single piece of decorative drama. In one bedroom, an antique mirror and painting have been set into a painted and gilded frame. The other has plain terracotta floors, trompe l'oeil dado panelling and an extravagant flourish in the form of a carved and gilded piece of religious ornament.**

Far right **Le Pavillon St Lambert, with its beautifully proportioned façade and formal gardens, replete with clipped box and beds of white roses, is classical heaven, and sits as placid and still as when it was built, more than 200 years ago.**

Right **Its infinity swimming pool, flanked by the arches of an orangery used as an outdoor dining area, has a view to the gardens beyond, through olive groves, where the trees are underplanted with lavender.**

refined luxury

Fit for a king – or for a king's sport, at least – Le Pavillon St Lambert was built in the 17th century and extended in the 18th century for a proposed visit by Louis XV. Two hundred years later, it was restored to its former charm and glory by a British interior designer, Blahnaid Behan.

In 17th-century France, the hunting lodge was a popular architectural form, often compact and classical in design and situated in a relatively isolated area, thereby allowing prolonged exposure to the many and varied pleasures of the hunt. Le Pavillon St Lambert is a hunting lodge of the period, a perfectly proportioned classical house, of a type still to be found in the clearings of the ancient forests south of Paris. But this lodge is far from Paris – about an hour from Aix-en-Provence, in the mountainous Luberon area, north of the villages of Bonnieux and Menèrbes, which featured in Peter Mayle's books about Provence. Built in the 17th century, it was extended and improved in the early 18th, in readiness for a visit by the French king, Louis XV. Le Pavillon

This page **The kitchen is clearly an all-important part of a house such as this, and Blahnaid has succeeded in equipping and building it as a state-of-the-art powerbase, while designing it to look as if it has merely been updated somewhat. The stone sinks, painted wooden units and woodwork, storage baskets, an oversized butcher's block and** **a completely modern cooking range combine to make this a perfect working room.**

Opposite **An inner hall leads from the central hall and metal-balustraded staircase. The room revels in a huge stone fireplace, a large painted armoire to hold glasses and plates, and local limestone flags on the floor.**

is a secret place – so secret, in fact, that when the interior designer Blahnaid Behan was beginning the enormous task of its restoration, and had contacted the relevant French conservation authorities, she discovered that they had no knowledge of its existence.

To begin at the beginning: Blahnaid had been looking for a house in Provence for some time. Given her profession, she was keen to find something that could be 'a project'. As soon as she came across the details of St Lambert in the local estate agent's – and even as he tried to dissuade her, crying 'a ruin, a ruin' – she was already on her way. 'The first time I went there, I fell in love with the magical situation – in

the middle of a valley, far from everywhere except a medieval chateau on the hillside above.' The house today consists of a central pavilion flanked on either side by wings, but when she bought it only the central section existed, although it was evident that there had once been wings. Traces of the original foundations were found, buried – and it was on these foundations that the reconstruction was based.

Putting such a house back together was not easy – particularly when every detail, from the right stone for the floors (local limestone from Tarascon, and mosaics rescued from a demolished chateau) to the authentic windows and the restored *gypseries* (mouldings) in the

Right and above **The salon is a magnificent room, opening into the dining room, and Blahnaid has made the most of its fine proportions. The bare floor, the simple, typically French colour scheme of pale greys and soft whites, and the plain lines of the classical furniture – most of it found at fairs and specialist shops – make a fitting backdrop for the restored, elaborate plaster gypseries. The great surprise was the large-scale bas-relief stone fountain; it had been hidden and was found, carefully packed in straw, during the dismantling of the partitions that once divided up the salon into separate rooms.**

Left *The ground floor consists of a salon, a summer and winter dining room, a kitchen and the library–study shown here, decorated in the same soft colours as the rest of the house. The view through the French windows is of a classical statue framed in foliage. In this room, as elsewhere in the house, textiles are used to complement the decoration and architecture; linen and silk in understated tones echo the greys, pinks and satisfyingly French green-blues of the walls.*

Above *Every light fitting and lamp has been chosen to echo the style and period of the original house. This pair of table lamps are inspired by candle-holders of the period.*

salon was restored and re-made with great care and delicacy. Eventually, after several major setbacks, including the aftermath of a serious flood that meant that the newly laid terrace had to be broken up in order to install new, industrial-sized drains beneath – it was finished. The pavilion now consists of a large salon and summer and winter dining rooms, as well as a library and kitchen, on the ground floor. There are three double bedrooms above and a further two on the ground floor, as well as others in restored outbuildings. Although it looks like a perfect piece of period restoration, it lacks none of the domestic comforts of the 21st century such as underfloor heating (it can be very cold during the winter months) and efficient plumbing – all of which are hidden discreetly within the fabric of the house.

When one has had to undertake so much basic construction work and renovation – often the parts that other people find most difficult – the decoration and choice of furniture can seem almost easy in comparison. 'I wanted it to be comfortable, rather than museum-like, and yet reflect the period,' Blahnaid explains. Her own style is

*Right **Based on a traditional** lit à la polonaise, **this four-poster bed has been dressed in a quirky contemporary style, with linen and silks draped in a deliberately casual manner.***

*Below **The painted French chest of drawers is very much in keeping with the other pieces of furniture in the bedroom.***

*Opposite, above and below **An Italian marble bathtub graces the en suite bathroom; on the wall hangs an unusually narrow pair of mirrors. The round bowl of a basin has a contemporary look but, equally, appears as if it might have been left abandoned in the old house.***

pared-down and relatively simple with clean lines and cool colour, and she wanted to bring this modern discipline to the interior decoration. So she furnished the house with a mixture of antiques and classical modern pieces. She found antiques of the period wherever she could – by chance, Le Pavillon is not far from L'Isle-sur-la-Sorgue, mecca for antique lovers from all over Europe and always a useful shopping destination. Overall, she found many treasures, particularly in the bed department – two bedrooms now boast wonderful *lits à la polonaise* – as well as other evocative pieces of decorative furniture and objects.

Textiles were chosen with equal care to be simple, yet luxurious – mainly silks, satins and linen in subdued and subtle colours. Actually, all the colours are genuinely subtle. 'I wanted to achieve an effect of tone on tone, each room flowing into the next through colour as well

as architecturally. I had a wonderful team of artists and each room was worked on like a canvas until we achieved the correct tones.'

There was also the problem of the garden. As with the house, very little remained above ground, and there was scant archival evidence of what had gone before. But excavation showed the whereabouts of both an old moat and a formal garden with the remnants of stone irrigation canals. On the basis of such slender clues, Blathnaid was able to plan and plant not only a formal garden of the period, but also an Italianate blue and white garden, as well as a rose garden and olive and lavender groves. Out of sight of the house is a two-tiered infinity swimming pool, with views over the endless countryside.

One feels that, if King Louis XV revisited Le Pavillon St Lambert today, there is a strong possibility that he might never leave.

eclectic

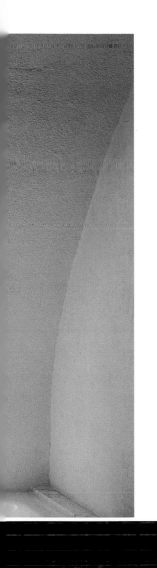

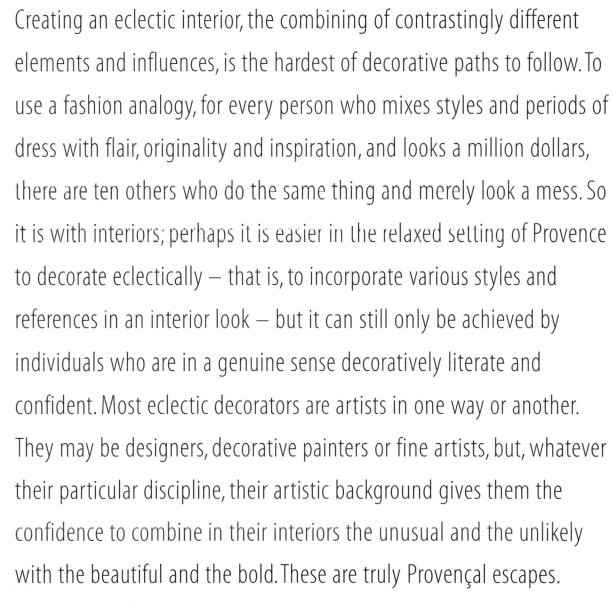

Creating an eclectic interior, the combining of contrastingly different elements and influences, is the hardest of decorative paths to follow. To use a fashion analogy, for every person who mixes styles and periods of dress with flair, originality and inspiration, and looks a million dollars, there are ten others who do the same thing and merely look a mess. So it is with interiors; perhaps it is easier in the relaxed setting of Provence to decorate eclectically – that is, to incorporate various styles and references in an interior look – but it can still only be achieved by individuals who are in a genuine sense decoratively literate and confident. Most eclectic decorators are artists in one way or another. They may be designers, decorative painters or fine artists, but, whatever their particular discipline, their artistic background gives them the confidence to combine in their interiors the unusual and the unlikely with the beautiful and the bold. These are truly Provençal escapes.

Right The bastide *incorporates clever use of colour and the decorative arts with imagination and skill. In an upstairs room, for example, pictures are displayed along the front of a fabric-lined armoire, stacked one on top of the other and propped up on the floor below – all changed around on a regular basis.*

Far right *Colour has been used throughout the house to create a series of artistic compositions. In this corner, no other element is needed to complement the green-painted cupboard door, the blue-washed door and the terracotta walls.*

an artistic masterpiece

Of all the many beautiful areas in Provence, one of the most evocative is the ancient city of Arles and the strange, often wild countryside that surrounds it. The quality of the light there – so much admired by, among others, Vincent Van Gogh – seems even more luminous and clear than elsewhere in Provence.

The area around Arles is the province of artists, which is perhaps why Irene Silvagni and her artist husband, Giorgio, live there. Their house – a solid, rambling *bastide* – is hidden away in a village outside the city, where the air is warm and the trees are thick. Giorgio Silvagni has transformed it into a place full of surprises, where colour is used not as a decorating device or a space divider but as a central character in the drama of the decoration. Around every corner is something new or unexpected. Yet to the Silvagnis there is a logical pattern; everything is there for a reason, and nothing is necessarily the same for ever.

This page **The Silvagnis collect** [...] *new and old pottery made in Vallauris, and they use and display it constantly. The rubbed terracotta walls act as a fine backdrop for the pottery as well as for the painted table and chairs. Quirky touches include the wall-hung, wrought-iron table – made by Giorgio – that* [...] *life as an ornamental balcony in Spain before being hammered into its present form.*

Opposite **The combined kitchen** *and dining room extends across one part of the ground floor; at each end is a door opening into a courtyard. The room is simple in the extreme and, as usual in this house, colour is the defining element of the decoration.*

Furniture is, on the whole, solid and reassuring – chosen to suit both the house and the rural surroundings.

Through the main entrance is a striking living hall, created from what was once a courtyard, with an oversized fireplace and seats layered in old textiles. Half cobbled and half paved, its plaster walls coloured and distressed in deep, vibrant tones of red, the hall has an almost medieval appearance. By contrast, the other side of the house – where a combined kitchen and dining room can be found – has a pair of doors, one at each end, which open onto cool courtyards.

Upstairs, tall windows with unlined, lightweight curtains let in the breezes, while thick walls keep out the heat. The master bedroom is especially cool, in both senses of the word – as dramatic as the rooms downstairs, with bold paint effects on walls and furniture – but also extremely comfortable, with an upholstered bedhead draped in an old quilt and another quilt covering an inviting-looking chair. The mosquito net here has been dyed blue, and in another

Below **A slightly cooler, calmer atmosphere prevails on the upper floor – certainly along the corridors, where unlined curtains at the tall windows provide a shaded light while allowing the breeze to circulate through the bedrooms. One landing is graced by a pair of Italian plaited leather chairs from the 1950s.**

Above and right **Like the rest of the house, the bathrooms have a raffish, eccentric charm. This one combines various periods and styles, incorporating heavy full-length curtains, an ornate gilded mirror, an old wooden washstand and a chrome and leather 1930s dressing stool.**

bedroom a white mosquito net is hung from the ceiling behind the bed, like a classical coronet canopy. Along the upper floor, a wide landing leads to other rooms, many of which are arranged *enfilade*. Every room in the house is coloured in its totality, so that it is an artist's creation, taking in every decorative element from the walls to the furniture to the textiles. In one room, for example, a wall is painted in deep blue and white stripes, and an armoire against the wall has been incorporated into the scheme, with its wood divides painted white and panels lined with bright red fabric as a contrast to the surrounding walls. Perhaps inspired by the Silvagnis' collection of green-glazed Vallauris pottery, a store cupboard against a terracotta-coloured wall in the dining end of the kitchen has been painted a warm lime-olive green, while the outside door has been painted blue. Again, the whole scheme exhibits a masterly use of traditional colours and techniques, all put together in a completely original way.

Opposite *Against a wash of deep red plaster, the imposing chimney piece in the hall – once part of an outer courtyard – is garlanded with bargello-like tapestry pieces and crowned with a striking stone pediment. More textile remnants are piled in a basket next to the fire.*

This page *On one side of the room, a relatively simple, late 18th-century bench seat, has been covered with a Provençal fabric and draped with a boutis. In the corner is an oversized terracotta urn, reminiscent of a water pot and subtly blending with the red-toned plaster.*

Half cobbled and half paved, its plaster walls coloured and distressed in deep vibrant tones of red, the entrance hall has an almost medieval appearance.

As befits an artist, Giorgio makes his colours work hard. Not simply applied to the walls, they are layered, distressed, rubbed back and washed. Giorgio paints patterns over base colours, too – basic stripes, but also freehand designs, with flowers and leaves climbing over walls. Colour is also used to accentuate Irene's large and ever-increasing collection of textiles, which can be seen everywhere in the house – from the *boutis* (old quilts) over beds, chairs, sofas and tables to the unusual hangings and small fragments of interestingly patterned cottons and silks used as cushions. Even the fireplace in the hall has been draped with a couple of pieces of Bargello-like tapestry. Old textiles also make their way into the garden. Demonstrating a refreshing lack of respect for age or rarity, the cushions scattered around the pool are covered in old fabric fragments.

Furniture is, on the whole, solid and reassuring – chosen to suit both the house and the surroundings. Unlike much of the furniture to be found in this part of France, the pieces are neither particularly Provençal nor particularly of a single period. The 20th century is as much admired in the Silvagni household as the

Right and above **In common with all other Provençal dwellers, the Silvagnis treat the outside spaces as an extension of those indoors. Scattered around the garden are tables in sheltered and shaded spots, one overlit by an alfresco variation on the ceiling light. Another, in almost African mode, is set beneath a pergola with a split cane blind hanging behind a bench draped with ethnic textiles. The warm colours and patterns of the fabrics are echoed in the table itself, which has been brightly painted with bold designs.**

Far right **The colour palette and rustic patterning are even echoed in the pottery plates.**

18th century, and country designs mix happily with more urban styles. They are not precious, pampered pieces, but chosen to suit each particular room – and often painted with abandon to enter into the general scheme of things. There are quirky, unusual elements, too, which show the extent of the Silvagnis' imagination, such as the wrought-iron console table attached to the wall in the kitchen – which is, in fact, an old iron balcony found in a Spanish house, recycled and given an entirely new life by Giorgio.

The garden is as mysterious as the house. Almost overgrown, with an air of being a hidden secret, it includes a swimming pool designed to look as if it had always been there and a dining table beneath a shady tree lit by a fantastical outdoor chandelier.

Nothing is expected, yet all is familiar and utterly comfortable – an effect which is difficult to achieve, and depends not only on Giorgio and Irene's decorative skills but also on their total understanding of the spirit of their beautiful old house.

Right **The house has a typically Provençal colour scheme and much has been made of the indoor/outdoor relationship. The owner has brought the garden to the house, growing vines and plants thickly up the walls and building a pergola close to an outdoor grill and barbecue.**

Left and above **An ideal place to enjoy a cup of coffee or a glass of wine, this wooden bench is dressed with a checked seat cushion and an assortment of floral-printed cotton cushions.**

a charming confection

Hélène Louise has decorated her house, inside and out, so that it appears to merge seamlessly with the outdoor space. The façade is the perfect Provençal combination – pale pink limewash with soft-green shutters and with a fairytale pergola shading a curly metal dining table and chairs.

Hélène Louise, the daughter of the owners of Le Vieux Jas (see pages 68–75), has an instinctive love of the Provençal countryside. She has had her own house, close to that of her parents, for about three years, and it is instructive to see how she has interpreted the taste and style inherited from an earlier generation, retaining much and yet simplifying and editing to create a fresh look that is entirely of today. When the family found the

house – a building based on a central core that is now the hall – there was much to do. Over the past few years they have turned it into a much larger and very comfortable house with views over valleys and hills to the city of Aix in the distance.

As in all good French homes, the heart of the place is the kitchen, which successfully mixes old and new. A 19th-century marble sink looks like a state-of-the-art

contemporary work, and a huge cupboard, built to store spices and provisions, is used to display Hélène Louise's collection of coffee jugs, pitchers, terrines and relief-moulded Barbotine ceramics. A mélange of antique patterned tiles make a patchwork on the walls, running behind the new range and the old sink. The practical table is an old one with a marble top, and the chairs are traditional woven French café chairs.

Hélène Louise's tastes reflect her mother's most clearly in the living room. There are the same warm tones of pink and deeper pink as in the parents' home, the same clever use of textiles, mixing pattern and

This page *A double marble sink is set above a storage area curtained off with old French linen. There is a patchwork of 19th-century patterned tiles behind the sink and the range – which is new but retains a period feel. In the corner is a pizza oven, with a border of leaping fish around the brick edges, and traditional pottery bowls and egg cups are stacked decoratively on open shelves.*

Above **A large, glass-doored** meuble d'épicerie *holds a wide variety of china pieces, ranging from terrine dishes and jugs to some relief-moulded Barbotine ceramics. Next to the cupboard, a stand from a stationery shop is used to display a collection of postcards, and on the table is a set of old, marble-based scales.*

It is a pleasing mix of old and new; that which is new has a passing resemblance to the old, and that which is old appears perfectly chosen and perfectly placed.

Above **Beside the Florentine cupboard that once belonged to Hélène's grandfather is a wood-framed day bed from the 1930s, which was found in a hotel and reupholstered by Hélène.**

Right **The 19th-century screen in the corner of this bedroom has been rehung with textiles from Hélène's collection.**

Above right **The red sofa in the living room dates from the time of Napoleon III, while the shelf in the corner, used to display a bust, was found in a pharmacy.**

Above far right **The mix of fabrics, including the screen with its painted wood frame and panels covered in a floral stripe, makes a harmonious picture.**

colour in practised mode. 'I wanted to arrange the furniture in the living room to make several small areas, separated by textiles,' says Hélène Louise. Beautiful textiles are everywhere – covering sofas, daybeds and chairs, and in the guise of cushions, throws and draped *boutis*, or traditional quilts. She has used unlined white curtains at the French windows, which set off her other antique fabrics to perfection and give the room an air of freshness and simplicity.

Upstairs in the four bedrooms Hélène Louise has again combined antique furniture, used in a modern way, with simple backgrounds. In one room are traditional Napoleon III Italian beds with shaped metal headboards which were originally painted black; by repainting them Hélène has lifted and transformed them into something pretty and modern. The Italian wooden bench at the end of the bed, originally from a church, has also been painted to complement the bed behind.

She wanted to ensure a natural movement between the inside and the outside. To that end, tall French windows stand open to a garden filled with fruit trees and roses, vines and olives, chestnut and box. There are shaded arbours and sunny pockets. As in the house, there are different areas linked with skill; and, as in the house, there is a freshness and directness about it all that cannot fail to charm.

This page and opposite **Maurizio** *Epifani has restored this former farmworker's dwelling with as light a hand as possible. In the airy living room, for example, there is comfort, there is style – and there is also simplicity. Well-upholstered chairs and sofas sit next to choice 18th-century pieces – 'poor French furniture', as Maurizio calls it. Both walls and upholstery are neutral in tone, enlivened with cushions made from old textiles and the odd galloping horse.*

spare and sophisticated

A peasant's house outside Grasse, dating from the 17th century, has been restored by antique dealer Maurizio Epifani. 'Old houses should be left in their original state as far as possible,' he says, 'and there should never be heavy restructuring of the exterior, which should remain integral to the surrounding environment.'

Maurizio Epifani opened L'Oro dei Forlacchi, his antique shop in Milan, 15 years ago, when antique collecting and selling were still both traditional and conventional. Imagine, therefore, customers' surprise at a shop filled with fruit machines and 1950s robots next to old Chinese chairs and Provençal armoires. The idea was, he says, to stock the 'improbable and the unlikely', and its success was both immediate and continuing.

So it is surprising that Maurizio's house in Provence, near Grasse, is minimal in style, with a sense of space and light that seems in complete contrast to his shop. Although the area is now well populated – and has been since the 19th century, when Grasse became the heart of the French perfume industry – it was once as sparsely populated as the rest of rural Provence.

Above **The kitchen is as light and airy as could be wished – white on white, with the witty touch of a ceramic, glazed bas-relief of a full-grown olive tree growing across the wall.**

Right and above right **If you live in Provence and have the space, it is always worth having both an outdoor and an indoor dining room. The latter is useful not only when it is too cold but also when it is too hot. The dining room in this house is conscious of its past incarnation, being a restored lean-to with a full-length cupboard for crockery, wide window openings carved out of the walls and a sloping beamed ceiling painted white.**

Maurizio's house – its core at any rate – dates from the 17th century and was the home of the peasant family who worked the land for the principal landowning family of the district. Over the years, various additions and alterations had been made – to the extent that, when Maurizio bought it four years ago, he felt that there was little major work to be done.

With his cultivated eye for the old and the antique, Maurizio has always felt strongly that the essence of the house should stay relatively intact. Equally crucial is not to try to change the house's character; it should remain in feeling as it was originally designed – or, as Maurizio puts it, 'Don't try to transform an old country house into a castle.' With this in mind, he tried to do minimal work on the interior. The main changes were installing a staircase to link the first-floor living room with the garden and the addition of two bathrooms.

Inside, the house is almost austere in its simplicity. Each room is painted in the softest of whites. There is little contrast. Beams and woodwork are painted in the same colours as the walls, and the floors have neutral

Above **In the principal bedroom, there is little in the way of fabrics other than a heavy antique quilt on a bed dressed with white linen. The requisite 'animalier' element takes the form of a large painting of an elk propped against the wall.**

Opposite **The adjoining bathroom features a double wooden washstand, set with two basins and lit, unexpectedly, with two table lamps at each end of the upper shelf.**

coverings. This plain background allows him to include interesting pieces of furniture, much of it from the 18th century: 'poor French furniture', as he calls it – that is, simple country furniture as opposed to grand pieces. Against these pieces, he adds flashes of colour and unusual details, as in the airy living room, where the plain French windows are flanked by waxed wooden carved pilasters rather than curtains. The same windows are crowned by a prancing wooden horse, one of his collection of '*animalier*' objects. This is in accord

with his views on how the interiors of old houses should be treated: 'For the interior, if it has to be refurbished, old materials only should be used, or – if that is not possible – materials that are as similar as possible to the original, such as recycled old wooden flooring, old stone, old fireplaces and so on.' Textiles also come within this strict remit. They are usually thick linens, often old and second-hand, and in natural colours – beiges, dusty blues, faded greens, and 'always, always white'. This natural simplicity is important to Maurizio: 'Never

This page and opposite The garden design and the choice of plants are as important as the arrangement of the rooms. As well as olive trees, *Arbutus unedo* and a grape vine growing up the front of the house, there is an airy pergola, supporting kiwi-fruit trees. Beneath it is a dining table on a terracotta tiled terrace, looking towards a swimming pool designed in classical style, with a raised edge like a formal canal. Behind the pool is a stag at rest, set against a backdrop of greenery, almost as if he were alive.

be excessive with the decoration. Too many fabrics are detrimental – like curtains and bedspreads with heavy patterns, florals, little *ton-sur-ton* sets.' An overload of pattern can make an otherwise plain interior seem fussy, and in an often hot climate it is essential that inside the house seem as cool and quiet as possible.

The kitchen is as simple as the drawing room – again, it is all white, and the central decorative motif is a subtle white ceramic rendition of an olive tree, which grows upwards, spreading its branches and leaves across the wall.

Garden life is important here. The indoor dining room is surrounded by greenery, while the outside dining area is a long terrace running along one side of the house. When Maurizio bought the house, the swimming pool was already there, complete with the additional wing, which he has made into a guest house: 'I have not done much to that area, other than refresh it, lighten the surroundings and add the bronze deer to overlook the pool.' A garden designer, Stefano Baccari, was enlisted to 'modify' the rest of the garden, refining the plant and vegetative life to exclude species that were not native to the area.

The final result is a charming combination of the simple and the sophisticated, with something to look at, at every turn – very similar, perhaps, to the sensation felt by collectors at L'Oro dei Farlocchi.

Main picture *Built as an adjunct to a neighbouring 18th-century hunting lodge, the pavilion has the settled appearance both of old age and no age, with its classical heavy stone lintels and wide glass fanlights.*

Inset *The double doors open into an entrance hall covered in the vibrant, madder-toned toile de Jouy, La Toile Villageoise, which makes the space look larger than it is. At the far end is a spiral mahogany staircase; a section of the beamed ceiling is removable in order to pass furniture between floors.*

fairytale pavilion

The American decorator Kenyon Kramer lives outside Aix-en-Provence in a perfect classical pavilion – which isn't actually classical at all. The story of how it came into existence is very French – almost worthy of a *conte de fées* by the French teller of fairytales, Charles Perrault.

Kenyon Kramer works in Aix-en-Provence with the renowned French interior and landscape designer Jean-Louis Raynaud. Like most successful designers, Jean-Louis is a man who knows what he likes, and when he spotted near Carpentras – about 80 miles from Aix – a ruined 18th-century hunting lodge, built by a former Archbishop of Avignon, he knew that he liked it and wanted it – but not there. So he bought it and transported it stone by stone to a field near Aix, where he rebuilt it to its former glory, surrounding it with a fine garden.

All that it lacked was the pair of pavilions that usually flanked a lodge of that period. Happily, Aix is filled with beautiful buildings from the 17th and 18th centuries, and it was not long before Jean-Louis noticed, either side of the spectacular Pavillon Vendôme, a pair of tiny gatehouses, beguiling but in a state of disrepair – the design of which would work wonderfully well with the hunting lodge. The gatehouses were obviously the answer, but this time, instead of uprooting them, Jean-Louis merely, after the requisite discussions with Le Commission

This page and opposite **The tiny ground floor of the pavilion is oddly seductive and enticing, and looks larger than it actually is – a look achieved in part by the ubiquitous use of the toile (in a warm shade; the classical grey-blue colourway would not have worked nearly as well). The other triumph is in the selection of objects, prints and furniture** **such as the dining chairs, once ballroom chairs, which are just the right proportions for the 1950s Jansen-designed tole table. The seamless use of toile – not only in curtains, cushions and walls but also on the banquette seat in the corner – eliminates the architectural stops and angles and extends the boundaries of the room.**

'It is the perfect house,' says Kenyon Kramer. 'Everyone who comes wants it; because the scale is so good, you feel good, and this is how you want to live.'

des Monuments Historiques, the body that cares for historic buildings, reproduced them as adjuncts to his main house. (After he had finished, the Monuments Historiques restored the originals – giving the fairy story a happy ending.) It is one of these pavilions, Le Pavillon de Levant, that Kenyon Kramer today calls home.

Gatehouses were never designed to be especially commodious, and this one is no exception. Before Kenyon added some practical essentials – of which more later – the pavilion consisted of a salon and hall on the ground floor with a pair of bedrooms above, the floors linked by a narrow mahogany spiral staircase in one corner. Small as it was, it had one great advantage over equally tiny but more modern buildings, in that its proportions, although miniature in scale, could not be bettered. As Kenyon says, 'It is the perfect cube, and therefore supremely comfortable to be in; because the proportions are good, you feel good in the space.'

It is an oft-repeated rule of good decorating that the smaller the space the larger the scale of the furnishings and the decoration should be. Following this maxim,

This page and opposite **The original pavilion was built without a kitchen, a state which American-born Kenyon had to change. Mindful of the disparity between classical elegance and modern practicality, he designed a glazed lean-to kitchen with dark green glazing bars that, from above, could be taken for a perfectly-in-period orangery. An American slate sink is set into a limestone worktop; in traditional Provençal fashion, the kitchen equipment is stored on shelves beneath the worktop, hidden by striped linen slotted onto metal curtain rods. The table, which also has a stone top, was specially made to fit the space.**

Kenyon decided to use the boldest of bold prints throughout, starting with Braquenié's traditional 'Tree of Life' design as bed hangings and cover in the main bedroom, and continuing down through the rest of the house with an exuberant toile de Jouy, also by Braquenié. In the salon, the Braquenié toile covers every surface. As is evident, this does not make the room feel small at all. Instead, the subtle, all-over two-tone design, coupled with the sobering, softening tones of the flat pea-green woodwork, gives the room a look of utter comfort and complete timelessness. Neither is the furniture chosen by Kenyon

Kramer what could be described as doll's-house scale. Everything is full-sized, including the Baldwin grand piano in the salon, but some subtle visual tricks have also been played; for example, instead of using sofas in the centre of the room, Kenyon has designed squashy, cushioned banquettes which sit neatly around the walls, loose-covered in yet more of the ubiquitous toile.

To return to the aforementioned practicalities: as Kenyon says, 'I'm an American – I need my kitchen and my bathroom.' But how to incorporate them both into the period design, without disturbing the

This page and opposite **Kenyon** *has pursued the same principles upstairs as on the ground floor. There are two bedrooms and a minuscule bathroom, carved from an existing dressing room to make an almost cabin-like space. Although not every wall is covered in toile – in the main bedroom, because the walls slope steeply, Kenyon decided to paint them a pale terracotta as a foil for the dramatic toile-draped period bateau-lit – the overall principle remains one of larger-than-life scale for a smaller-than-usual space; this is epitomized by the choice of bed as well as the other, rather masculine pieces of furniture.*

classical symmetry both inside and, equally importantly, from the outside too? The bathroom was relatively simple. Kenyon carved out a suitable space from what was already there: 'I cut a hole, almost an oval, from an existing dressing room.' This is now a cabin-like space complete with a shower and a smart bath panelled in deepest mahogany.

The kitchen presented more of a problem. Impossible to incorporate within the existing fabric, it required the building of an extension. Kenyon's solution was worthy of a 17th-century classical architect. Aware that any extension could be viewed, and found wanting, from the upper floors of the main house, he designed the lean-to kitchen with a glass roof, the whole inspired by period orangeries. All that can be seen from above are dark green glazing bars, with presumably the suggestion of potted lemon and orange trees within.

Now the work is finished, Kenyon is happy. 'It is the perfect house. Everyone who comes wants it; because the scale is so good, you feel good, and this is how you want to live.'

Left and right **Every cubic metre (yard) counts in this tiny house, so the owner, a self-confessed non-cook, has squeezed all the kitchen facilities she needs into a corner of the main living area. But although small, the kitchen is as charming as the rest of the house. As elsewhere, paint has been used to delineate the space. Instead of a border or a dado design as seen in the sitting room, she has created what amounts to a trompe l'oeil splashback behind the sink – which might possibly be made of tiles or granite, but instead is pure paint. A patchwork of Portuguese blue and white tiles across the small worktop continues the colour theme.**

seaside refuge

Standing 400 metres (yards) above the sea and looking down over it, this mini house in Ramatuelle is the hideaway of an Italian designer, for whom it provides peace and solitude – and a refuge from working life.

When contemplating the joys of Provençal life, it can be easy to forget that Provence – vast and varied area that it is – extends not only to the mountains of the Haut-Var but also to the sparkling Mediterranean Sea. For every dwelling with a view of lavender fields and olive groves, there is another with a view, however distant, of glittering water and the umbrella pines that sometimes extend nearly to the water itself – 'les pieds dans l'eau', as they say in the guidebooks.

Overlooking the Mediterranean from the village of Ramatuelle, this tiny house – only 7 metres (23 feet) deep and 2.5 metres (8 feet) wide – is adorned and furnished in the simplest of styles, but it is also a place of great charm. To make it a restful home that works well, enormous care was taken to plan everything in the most efficient and

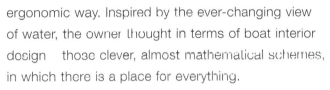

ergonomic way. Inspired by the ever-changing view of water, the owner thought in terms of boat interior design – those clever, almost mathematical schemes, in which there is a place for everything.

The minute, galley-like kitchen on the ground floor – whose size reflects the owner's lack of enthusiasm for cooking – is telescoped into a corner of the living area and decorated in the same soft tones as the rest of the room. On either side of the living area, against the walls, are seats consisting of thick, deep-buttoned mattresses piled high with cushions of various designs. They not only make suitably rustic and comfortable sofas but also double as instant beds for guests.

A narrow staircase leads up to a tiny bedroom, which resembles the forward cabin in a boat, with the bed set cosily underneath the angled beams of the roof; there is little space between bed and walls, but material draped either side adds softness.

Outside the bedroom is a terrace, large enough for one person, which, like the bedroom ceiling, is washed at night by the beam from the nearby lighthouse.

This page **An interior designer by profession, the owner has used her skill lightly here but with practised charm. Nothing shouts, yet all is arranged and presented in a disciplined way to make a harmonious whole. For example, in the living area, an old food safe, painted blue, has been wall-hung and used to store household linens.**

Opposite **Above a painted blue skirting board (baseboard), topped with a further narrow blue line – a continuation of the kitchen colour scheme – she has hung, very simply, a group of wire baskets. One is used in the way in which it was first intended; the others are arranged in purely decorative, and striking, manner.**

Above and above right **A faux nautical theme – deep sea blue, touched with red and white – is used throughout the house. Downstairs, hand-painted wall decoration, inspired by the Turkish carpet on the floor, is both ethnic and simple.**

Opposite **In the tiny bedroom, the same colours prevail. Lack** of space means that the bed is fitted beneath the sloping eaves – in true nautical fashion – and draped with a casually arranged curtain of blue and red.

Top **Even the bathroom could be at sea: a full-size bath cut in half and rearranged to fit the space is a concept that many a boat designer would envy.**

The tiny bathroom is a triumph of alternative thinking: an old French zinc bath has been literally cut in half and fashioned into a modern version of a Victorian hip bath; it is both practical and comfortable, and looks like the daybed of an eccentric inventor.

Since the house is so small, the owner has been careful to adopt a single, cohesive decorative scheme – one that was inspired by the natural surroundings. Blue and white, the colours of sea and sky, appear in each of the rooms, with a washed-out soft red used as accent and counterpoint.

She has painted the walls herself with simple, rather ethnic patterns, such as the dado design on the wall in the living room, whose colours were inspired by the Turkish carpet on the floor. For the kitchen counter, she has made a patchwork of antique Portuguese tiles – all blue and white, of course.

This is a summer house – it has no heating, and in the winter the winds can be biting and the air chill; but, when the mimosa is out and the air is soft, it is hard to imagine a more wonderful retreat.

business credits

architects, designers and properties featured in this book

BEHANDESIGN
44 Lansdowne Gardens
London SW8 2EF
tel: + 44 (0)7768 274 578
fax: + 44 (0)20 7498 7601
bbdltd@msn.com
www.behandesign.com
Pages 5, 108l, 109l, 136–45.

CAROLE OULHEN
Interior Designer
tel: + 33 6 80 99 66 16
fax: + 33 4 90 02 01 91
with the help of contractors:
Icardi Soditra Entreprise
tel: + 33 4 90 89 31 52
fax: + 33 4 90 87 72 14
icardi@wanadoo.fr
Pages 66b, 66–67b, 88–93.

CHATEAU DE GIGNAC
Gignac en Provence 84400
France
tel: + 33 4 90 04 84 33
www.gaspard-de-gignac.com
Pages 108ar, 109ar, 128–35.

COLLETT–ZARZYCKI LTD
Fernhead Studios
2B Fernhead Road
London W9 3ET
tel: + 44 (0)20 8969 6967
fax: + 44 (0)20 8960 6480
www.collett-zarzycki.com
Pages 2–4, 12br, 22–31.

DAISY SIMON INTERIORS
Architecte D'Intérieur Décoration
55 Cours Mirabeau
Passage Agard
13100 Aix-en-Provence
France
daisy.simonaix@wanadoo.fr
Pages 94–99.

ENRICA STABILE
Antiques dealer,
interior decorator and
photographic stylist
www.enricastabile.com
shop:
L'Utile e il Dilettevole
Via Carlo Maria Maggi 6
20154 Milan
Italy
tel: + 39 0234 53 60 86
Pages 6–7, 66al, 66ar, 76–83, 84–87, endpapers.

FRÉDÉRIC MÉCHICHE
4 rue de Thorigny
75003 Paris
France
tel: + 33 1 42 78 78 28
fax: + 33 1 42 78 23 30
Pages 10–11, 44–49.

FRENCH COUNTRY LIVING
Antiques & Decoration
21 rue de l'Eglise
06250 Mougins
France
tel: + 33 4 93 75 53 03
fax: + 33 4 93 75 63 03
f.c.l.com@wanadoo.fr
Pages 100–105.

HÉLÈNE LOUISE
Interior designer
Aix-en-Provence
France
tel: + 33 6 21 04 25 83
Pages 148bl, 160–65.

ISABELLE SCHOUTEN
Collection Privée Antiquités
www.collection-privee.com
Pages 1, 13ar, 50–57.

**KENYON KRAMER AND
JEAN-LOUIS RAYNAUD
ASSOCIATES**
Décoration et Jardins
3 Place des Trois Ormeaux
13100 Aix-en-Provence
France
tel: + 33 4 42 23 52 32
fax: + 33 4 42 23 29 07
Pages 8–9, 108br, 120–27, 148al, 148–49br, 149ar, 174–81.

L'ORO DEI FARLOCCHI
Via Madonnina fronte N° 5
Milan
Italy
tel: + 39 0286 05 89
www.lorodeifarlocchi.com
Pages 146–47, 148–49ar, 166–73.

NELLY GUYOT
Décoratrice
tel: + 33 6 09 25 20 68
Pages 12l, 13al, 14–21.

NICOLETTA MARAZZA
Interior designer
Milan
Italy
by appointment
tel: + 39 0276 01 44 82
Pages 182–87.

ROBERT DALLAS
tel: + 33 4 93 32 55 55
Pages 2–4, 12br, 22–31.

TITA BAY
Interior decorator
Via Sudorno 22D
24100 Bergamo
Italy
tel: + 39 0352 58 384
Pages 32–37.

VILLA MARIE
Ramatuelle
St Tropez
France
tel: + 33 4 94 97 40 22
fax: + 33 4 94 97 37 55
contact@villamarie.fr
www.c-h-m.com
Pages 106–107, 110–19.

photography credits

key: a=above, b=below, r=right, l=left, c=centre, ph=photographer.
All photographs by Christopher Drake unless otherwise stated.

Front endpapers Enrica Stabile's house in Le Thor, Provence; **page 1** a country house near Mougins, Provence; **2–4** designed by Andrzej Zarzycki for Collett–Zarzycki Ltd in association with Robert Dallas; **5** Le Pavillon St Lambert in the Luberon Valley, designed by Blathnaid Behan of Behandesign; **6–7** Enrica Stabile's house in Le Thor, Provence; **8–9** Mas de Source Cachée, private guesthouse in St Rémy de Provence, designed by Kenyon Kramer & Jean-Louis Raynaud; **10–11** ph Fritz von der Schulenburg/Frédéric Méchiche's house near Toulon; **12l** décoratrice Nelly Guyot's home; **12br** designed by Andrzej Zarzycki for Collett–Zarzycki Ltd in association with Robert Dallas; **13al** décoratrice Nelly Guyot's home; **13ar** a country house near Mougins, Provence; **14–21** décoratrice Nelly Guyot's home; **22–31** designed by Andrzej Zarzycki for Collett–Zarzycki Ltd in association with Robert Dallas; **32–37** Tita Bay's village house in Ramatuelle; **44–49** ph Fritz von der Schulenburg/ Frédéric Méchiche's house near Toulon; **50–57** a country house near Mougins, Provence; **58–63** ph Simon Upton; **64–65** Le Vieux Jas; **66al** Enrica Stabile's house in Le Thor, Provence; **66ar** Diana Bauer's house near Cotignac, styling by Enrica Stabile; **66b** & **66–67b** interior designer Carole Oulhen; **67ar** Le Vieux Jas; **68–75** Le Vieux Jas; **76–83** Enrica Stabile's house in Le Thor, Provence; **84–87** Diana Bauer's house near Cotignac, styling by Enrica Stabile; **88–93** interior designer Carole Oulhen; **94–99** a family home near Aix-en-Provence with interior design by Daisy Simon; **100–105** owners of French Country Living, the Hill family's home on the Côte d'Azur; **106–107** Villa Marie, Ramatuelle, St Tropez; **108l** Le Pavillon St Lambert in the Luberon Valley, designed by Blathnaid Behan of Behandesign; **108br** Mas de Source Cachée, private guesthouse in St Rémy de Provence, designed by Kenyon Kramer & Jean-Louis Raynaud; **108ar** & **109ar** the Chateau de Gignac, Michelle Joubert's home in Provence; **109l** Le Pavillon St Lambert in the Luberon Valley, designed by Blathnaid Behan of Behandesign; **110–19** Villa Marie, Ramatuelle, St Tropez; **120–27** Mas de Source Cachée, private guesthouse in St Rémy de Provence, designed by Kenyon Kramer & Jean-Louis Raynaud; **128–35** the Chateau de Gignac, Michelle Joubert's home in Provence; **136–45** Le Pavillon St Lambert in the Luberon Valley, designed by Blathnaid Behan of Behandesign; **146–47** Maurizio Epifani, owner of L'Oro dei Farlocchi; **148al**, **148–49br** & **149ar** Pavillon de Levant, gate house on the property of Pavillon de Victoire, Verneques, France, designed by Kenyon Kramer & Jean-Louis Raynaud; **148bl** Hélène Louise, interior designer; **148–49ar** Maurizio Epifani, owner of L'Oro dei Farlocchi; **150–59** Irene & Giorgio Silvagni's house in Provence: **150–57** ph Fritz von der Schulenburg; **160–65** Hélène Louise, interior designer; **166–73** Maurizio Epifani, owner of L'Oro dei Farlocchi; **174–81** Pavillon de Levant, gate house on the property of Pavillon de Victoire, Verneques, France, designed by Kenyon Kramer & Jean-Louis Raynaud; **182–87** a house in Ramatuelle, St Tropez; **back endpapers** Diana Bauer's house near Cotignac, styling by Enrica Stabile.

The publishers would like to thank all those who allowed us to photograph their homes for this book and who made us so welcome throughout each shoot. Many thanks to Enrica Stabile, Dominique Lubar of IPL Interiors and Kenyon Kramer for their help with research, and also to Jocelyne and Jean-Louis Sibuet at Villa Marie, Ramatuelle, for kindly allowing us to stay with them.

index

Page numbers in *italics* refer to illustrations.